"Can our preaching be exposi O'Neill answers yes by explaini ing. The book is wonderfully clear and full of helpful illustrations and practical advice. A helpful read for every preacher!"

Thomas R. Schreiner
James Buchanan Harrison Professor of New Testament Interpretation and professor of biblical theology, The Southern Baptist Theological Seminary

"In his insightful book on preaching, Lucas O'Neill brings together a variety of disciplines and experiences into a unified and practical approach that will help any preacher—whether you're still in seminary or have been preaching for 20 years. For those that desire to grow in their ability to be both faithful to Scripture and command the attention of their hearers, this is the book for you."

Julius J. Kim
Dean of students and professor of practical theology, Westminster Theological Seminary (California); author of *Preaching the Whole Counsel of God: Design and Deliver Gospel-Centered Sermons*

"If you are a preacher, tension is your friend, not your enemy. In fact, if your sermon lacks tension, people will stop listening—even if you are not finished preaching. Fortunately, as Lucas O'Neill argues, expository preaching and engaging preaching are not mutually exclusive. This volume will help you harness the power of tension in your preaching to command the attention of your listeners. There are no gimmicks here. O'Neill's strategy reflects how the Bible itself communicates its message. For the good of your listeners and the glory of God, take and read this book. Then put it into practice."

Steven D. Mathewson
Author of *The Art of Preaching Old Testament Narrative* and *Preaching the Four Gospels with Confidence*

"*Preaching to Be Heard* bridges the gap between the biblical text and communicating the truth of the text to one's listeners. A preacher's commitment to the idea of the text is complemented by solid delivery in the preaching of the sermon. This book demonstrates that these two dynamics in preaching are not in opposition to each other but are together vital for excellent preaching."

Scott M. Gibson

David E. Garland Chair of Preaching and director of the PhD in Preaching Program, Baylor University/ Truett Seminary (Waco, TX)

"Do you ever struggle with gaining—and then maintaining—the attention of your audience when preaching? I suspect all of us have at times! If that's you—or if it's something you wrestle with on a regular basis—let me commend Lucas O'Neill's book to you. Here you'll find some real help by means of creating and then maintaining tension in your sermons. Dr. O'Neill has done a marvelous job of developing out this concept as well as giving us a necessary refresher course on sermon structure to boot! I heartily recommend that Preaching to Be Heard be added to your reading list."

Scott A. Wenig

Haddon Robinson Chair of Biblical Preaching and Professor of Applied Theology, Denver Seminary

"What Bible teacher doesn't want to be heard? O'Neill's method to grab and sustain the attention of our listeners is simple: Teach Scripture. Scripture itself grabs interest by presenting tension, a need that requires resolution. He draws from other expositors' advice, gives examples for what he is driving at, and provides practice texts so the reader can try it for herself. I commend this useful resource to any woman Bible teacher who not only wants to be heard by her listeners, but wants the Bible to be heard."

Colleen J. McFadden

Director of Women's Workshops, The Charles Simeon Trust

"Lucas O'Neill aims to wipe out dull preaching. His remedy in *Preaching to Be Heard* goes deeper than efforts to garner vivid illustrations, tell heart-gripping stories, and design slick PowerPoint slides to "dress up" the message of a biblical text. Instead he calls preachers to dig into the life-changing agenda that God's Spirit has for his Word, and to draw in our listeners by conveying the tension, the suspense, in the passage itself. God's Word diagnoses every dimension of our brokenness, guilt, and enslavement; so our preaching commands and holds hearers' attention when we structure sermons to expose the specific aspect of our problem that each text addresses, signal the remedy that grace provides, and finally deliver the ultimate solution that is found in Christ and the power of his gospel. Abundant examples and helpful exercises make this book an excellent resource for preachers who long to see listeners absorbed in the drama of the Bible itself, and captivated by the Redeemer to whom Scripture witnesses on every page."

Dennis E. Johnson
Professor emeritus of practical theology,
Westminster Theological Seminary (California), author,
Him We Proclaim: Preaching Christ from All the Scriptures

"Expository preaching is fundamental to healthy preaching, a healthy understanding of the Bible, and a truly healthy church. But sound expository preaching that does not also engage the congregation leaves open the door for unhealthy churches—perhaps not because of the content, but because of a failure to communicate in a way that can be understood. For this reason, I am very grateful for this book. Every preacher who is serious about both the biblical content of his sermon and his congregation's understanding of that content will benefit from Lucas O'Neill's wise and faithful instruction."

Chris Bruno
Assistant professor of New Testament and Greek,
Bethlehem College and Seminary, author of *The Whole Story of the Bible in 16 Verses* and *The Whole Message of the Bible in 16 Words*

Preaching to Be Heard

Preaching to Be Heard

Delivering Sermons That Command Attention

Lucas O'Neill

Preaching to Be Heard: Delivering Sermons That Command Attention

Lexham Press, 1313 Commercial St., Bellingham, WA 98225
LexhamPress.com

Print ISBN 9781683592365
Digital ISBN 9781683592372

Lexham Editorial: Jennifer Edwards, Elliot Ritzema, and Christy Callahan
Cover Design: Jim LePage
Typesetting: Dovetail Publishing Services

To my wife, Tina: you are my crown (Prov 12:4).

And to my children, Raquel, Elias, Lincoln, and Elinor: you are truly my heritage and my reward (Ps 127:3).

Contents

Foreword

We are at an opportune moment in the teaching of homiletics. We are beyond the era of Puritan messages that devised a method to wring doctrine and duty from the topical comparisons of individual texts. We are beyond the acceptance of running commentaries that claimed to be expositions of texts—though they were little more than data dumps for theological hobbyists—or weekly penance for congregants whose consciences required that they go to a church that "focused on the Bible" regardless of its apparent applicability to their lives. Thankfully, we are also beyond the so-called New Homiletic that claimed to offer a pragmatic alternative to "textual preaching" through experiential understanding of the ethical themes of Scripture.

In the heyday of the New Homiletic, those identified as the "best guides" for the future of engaging preaching were those unwilling to acknowledge—and actually were opposed to acknowledging—the reality of transcendent truth. Many would not even concede the possibility of transferable truth, denying that we could *really* know another's meaning beyond our own experiential horizons.

Inductive and narrative methods driven by theories of human communication that rooted understanding in the shared experience of an existential moment were championed for their effectiveness in garnering the attention of listeners whose only measure of truth was self-significance. For the last three decades, homiletics instructors of every theological stripe joined the experimental methods of cordial and able scholars who convinced many that these methods, birthed in the waters of disbelief, could take precedence in proclaiming the message of God's word to those who believe.

No one can deny that there is much to learn about effective communication and the hermeneutics of understanding from those who investigate the dynamics of story, conversation, and experience. However, what got lost in the scholarship surrounding the New Homiletic was a commitment to revelation, authority, and the ability of the Holy Spirit to communicate unchanging truth from the divinely inspired word, rightly divided.

As a consequence, the discipline of homiletics increasingly became an exercise in substituting

- Experience for Transcendence
- Relating for Revelation
- Engagement for Exposition
- Technique for Truth
- Style for Substance

In light of these dynamics, and in faithfulness to their calling to teach others to expound the Scriptures as God's word to us, a new generation of evangelical teachers of preaching is rising across all cultures, nations, and ethnicities that reasserts the Scriptures will garner appropriate attention if biblical exposition is rightly defined and practiced. Expository preaching is finding a new hearing and new advocates in those who not only believe that the best preaching involves the explanation *and* application (revealing meaning and significance) of biblical texts, but also believe that such preaching is the best method of holding the attention and transforming the lives of those in whom the Holy Spirit is active. With this book, Lucas O'Neill shows himself to be among the ranks of those who believe the word of God is bread for which the people of God yearn, if preachers treat it and them with the understanding Scripture itself teaches.

Such an understanding does not deny the importance of learning how to communicate content to a narrative-oriented culture or how to be faithful to the various genres of Scripture in form as well as in content. The prophets and apostles learned and used conventions of communication that helped their words penetrate the minds and hearts of those to whom they preached. We should remain willing and desirous of learning dynamics of preaching effectiveness, but we are healthiest when our *emphasis* is on communicating the faith once-for-all delivered to the saints—not simply engaging listeners with their own versions of truth.

Every generation of Bible-believing preachers must relearn that when truth is downplayed as our primary concern in preaching, then technique becomes ascendant, and when technique becomes our focus, then we and our people lose confidence in the unique power of the word. The Holy Spirit who gave it is the same Spirit who indwells us to receive it, making God's truth both culturally transcendent and personally communicable.

Always, always we seesaw our discussions in this discipline of homiletics between an emphasis on *veritas* versus vehicle. Both are important, both are vital, but when preachers (and their teachers) *prioritize* how to derive and deliver content, rather than who has the best delivery or most winsome technique, then we serve the church best.

At this time, the discussions and debates in evangelical homiletics are more about content and how it is framed within the redemptive flow of Scripture. In part this is because the narrative/inductive enterprises have largely been spent without producing the spiritual fruit they promised in many evangelical and most mainline churches. Since that movement is "past-crest," we are now not as influenced by it, nor do we feel the same pressure to bow to it, in order to be credible in the academic ranks. Hopefully, this clears the field for more pressing and significant debates—as uncomfortable as they may be for determining the particulars and scope of our textual priorities—about how best to be faithful to the proclamation of God's authoritative word in both its particular and redemptive contexts. In these conversations, the best of our homiletics scholarship is devoting itself to

- Truth over Technique
- Content over Charm
- *Veritas* over Vehicle
- Redemptive Goals over mere Rhetoric or Rules

Our belief in the efficacy and power of the word preached binds us to the priority of exposition, not primarily to the craft of engagement. For a new generation of homiletics instructors such as Lucas O'Neill who are saying and teaching this, I am deeply grateful and profoundly hopeful.

Bryan Chapell
Pastor, Grace Presbyterian Church (Peoria, IL)
July 2018

Preface

Preachers face a difficult task. Each Sunday we have to teach the Bible to a distracted people. Today, a relentless blitz of information overwhelms our people's eyes and ears. All week long they are targeted by customized ads and pinged by their smartphones to check incoming messages, texts, updates, and calls. Communication is increasingly image based, articles are broken down into bite-sized pieces, and vlogs are even taking the place of blogs. Yet there we stand with an ancient text in our hands, asking our audiences to sit still for thirty to forty minutes while we talk.

But is technological advancement really to blame when people find our sermons boring? To be sure, our listeners more than ever suffer from attention overload. But it was still the '60s when Clyde Reid sought to understand why the pulpit was under widespread disparagement. He lamented that "most sermons today are boring, dull, and uninteresting. ... Whether we like to admit it or not, many persons feel that preaching today fails to capture their interest."[1] This was an issue long before we had social media or smartphone apps.

---

1. Clyde Reid, *The Empty Pulpit: A Study in Preaching as Communication* (New York: Harper & Row, 1967), 26.

Even earlier than Reid, in the '20s, Harry Emerson Fosdick penned his famous article "What Is the Matter with Preaching?" In it, he bemoaned what he perceived to be an epidemic in the pulpit of his time—sermons that fail to really engage the listener. There was little to be distracted with from our perspective. The problem was not the audience. These were people who took forever to do everything by today's standards. Comparatively speaking, they had incredible patience—but not for insipid preaching.

THE PROBLEM WITH OUR EXPECTATIONS

For those who think that a sermon should be focused on Scripture, it is easy to write off Fosdick's comments because he went on to disparage this kind of preaching in favor of a style that was more focused on the listener's needs. Yet I still think Fosdick's comments are tough to ignore. He was concerned with the flatness with which many preachers deliver their sermons, and we should be as well.

The problem has less to do with our audience and more to do with our expectations of them. Sure, people are very distracted. But people always have been. It is just difficult to sit and listen. We shouldn't expect people to listen simply because it is the word of God and it *ought* to be heard. Fosdick's issue with the preaching of his day was not just its high view of Scripture but its high view of the listener's interest. He entirely missed it on the first complaint but nailed the second. Preachers "take a passage from Scripture," he wrote, "proceeding on the assumption that the people attending church that morning are deeply concerned about what the passage means."[2] Now, mature Christians

2. Harry Emerson Fosdick, "What Is the Matter with Preaching?" reprinted from *Harper's Magazine* (July 1928), 133–41; in Mike Graves, ed. *What's the Matter with Preaching Today?* (Louisville: Westminster John Knox Press, 2004), 9.

should enter the church service with eager anticipation for God's word. But in reality, mature Christians are not always eager and, what's more, not all Christians are mature. Because preachers are expounding the words of God's special revelation, our listeners should be fully engaged every Sunday—the word of God is glorious! But this is what we must show our people rather than simply expect from them. As Craig Loscalzo has put it, "To expect a hearing just because you are 'the preacher' is naïve."[3]

Rather than assuming that the seats on Sunday morning are filled with people who are champing at the bit to hear God's word, we would do well to think through how we might get them there. We have the opportunity to bring the attention of our congregations to God's word. But we must seek to do this effectively. When listeners are disengaged, communication is not happening. We must earn their attention.

Communication scholar Lionel Crocker wrote about two kinds of attention: the kind that comes from effort and the kind that comes from interest.[4] The university professor who motivates students to listen attentively takes advantage of the fact that the students will receive a grade for the course. This is attention via effort. They are, in a sense, *forced* to listen. But Crocker argues that the speaker should aim for attention via *interest*. This taps into a person's natural mechanism for listening. If something is interesting, focus is easy and need not be forced. According to Crocker, "It is futile for the speaker to say 'They *ought* to listen to this.'"[5] The speaker should win attention

---

3. Craig A. Loscalzo, *Preaching Sermons That Connect: Effective Communication through Identification* (Downers Grove, IL: InterVarsity Press, 1992), 17.

4. Lionel Crocker, *Public Speaking for College Students*, 3rd ed. (New York: American Book Company, 1956), 223.

5. Ibid.

by demonstrating that what is being communicated is inherently interesting. Now, for the preacher expounding Scripture it is true—what subject matter is more vital to anyone than what God has revealed in the Bible? But this is precisely what we must convince our congregations to believe and remind them of each time.

As preachers, we need to help our listeners understand that they are not at church to merely sit through a talk. And they aren't to listen simply because it is the spiritual thing to do. They are here to receive a word from God and there is nothing more significant or relevant in the world. They may not understand this in the moment we begin to preach. But there is a way to win their attention via interest, focus it on a passage of Scripture, and sustain that engagement throughout the sermon. That's what this book is about.

PREACHING THAT IS WORTHY OF ATTENTION

Before delving into the process of maintaining an audience's attention, I must square away an important item: not every sermon is worth hearing. Many sermons are like meals from typical fast-food chains—flavor at the expense of nutrition. It's easy, fast, cheap, and tastes addictively good. Your preaching may be drawing a lot of people, but are they being fed well? It's easy to master the art of drawing an audience. If we give them something pleasantly palatable we can fill empty seats. But if we don't supply nutritious meals it is the people that are left empty.

I believe sermons that actually nourish souls are sermons that explain what a portion of Scripture means. This is called expository preaching. It is simply "that preaching which takes for the point of a sermon the point of a particular passage of

Scripture. That's it."[6] In it, preachers begin with a text and look for the point rather than begin with a point and look for a text to support it. This means we do not begin our preparation with the end in mind. We begin with the text and we surrender the sermon to its dictates. But we must say more. Expository preachers do not only communicate the point of the text, but they stick to the passage throughout the entire sermon. Everything in the sermon serves to shed light on the passage and what it communicates. This is preaching in its most ideal form.

Preachers who abandon exposition do not always do so intentionally. They do not always begin with a desire to scrap what Scripture says. It may be a lack of wisdom or training. It may be a lack of experience (how many of us wish we could take back some of our earliest sermons!). But there are preachers who know better, and perhaps there are more in this category than we might care to admit. They have forsaken a conviction to say what the text says and instead embark on a weekly search for something "that'll preach." Many preachers who get it wrong still have a respect and even a level of reverence for Scripture—they believe it is God's word. But they do not give it primacy in their preaching. This is because they begin by asking the wrong question.

It is wrongheaded to begin the sermon process by asking, "What do I want to say?" The question must be, "What does this Scripture passage say?" The expository preacher wants to find the intent of a particular passage in the Bible and preach that. This is not to say expositors should turn a blind eye to what people are feeling. Indeed, even the most anchored expositor

6. Mark Dever, *Nine Marks of a Healthy Church* (Wheaton, IL: Crossway, 2004), 40.

must surely think of the listeners' needs when deciding which text to preach or which book of the Bible to begin working through. It is good for the preacher to factor the particularities of any audience into the sermon planning process. This is why Paul's sermon to the crowd in the Areopagus (Acts 17) showed a different approach than his sermon to his audience in Pisidian Antioch (Acts 13). But being mindful of needs is altogether different than making those needs the starting point. The text, inspired by the Holy Spirit, must remain in the driver's seat. Not the needs perceived by the audience.

Truthfully, even if preachers could determine what is really happening in the minds and hearts of the people before them, the needs would not be uniform across the audience. Each person will have their own thoughts, their own struggles, their own perspectives. To push it further still, we must not assume that the listeners themselves have an accurate perception as to what their needs really are. "The heart is deceitful above all things, and desperately sick; who can understand it?" (Jer 17:9). At the end of the day, preachers who begin with the felt needs of the audience are really basing their sermons on what they perceive the listeners perceive their needs to be. Would it not be better to begin with Scripture? To believe that the Lord alone is able to "search the heart and test the mind" (v. 10)? To trust that these God-breathed words can make anyone in any situation complete and equipped for every good work (2 Tim 3:16)?

I met a young man who had recently finished a degree in ministry at a renowned evangelical theological school. Until his conversation with me, he had never heard of "expository preaching." Students pour into seminaries, many of them having learned what they know about preaching from their felt-needs pastors back home. If we are not clear about the need for sound exposition, we are handing our churches over to a generation of pastors who have a better understanding of mailers and seating dynamics than they do of God's word. We are starving our churches to death.

When I have taught introductory courses in preaching, I have typically begun with a definition of expository preaching and then a host of reasons why preaching must be done in this way.[7] If students can grasp how much is really at stake, it could be that more of them will carry a commitment to exposition with them into their ministries. Sermons must be engaging—we want to help audiences lend their attention to Scripture, and that is the purpose of this book. But attention doesn't matter if what they are attending to is not a careful examination of Scripture. Fortunately, we do not need to digress from Scripture in order to make an expositional sermon engaging.

WINNING ATTENTION WITH THE TEXT

The strategy for holding your listeners' attention that I share in the following pages is not the only one. But it is effective. It is a versatile approach that will keep the sermon varied, the preacher fresh, and the audience engaged. Most importantly, it is an approach to preaching that seeks to command attention *with* the biblical text, not in spite of it. The preacher's exegetical work is key, not incidental. When this approach to preaching began to take shape in my ministry, I was looking for a way to engage the audience while still keeping exposition primary. I assumed that one might compromise the other if I wasn't careful. But I have come to discover that this approach in fact underscores exposition because it is the text of Scripture itself that provides the object of interest.

---

7. You can find these biblical reasons in Appendix A: Resolving to Preach Expositionally, on page 173. That appendix also includes a self-exam to help you determine whether you are preaching expositionally.

In this book, I want to argue that there is nothing more relevant, awe-inspiring, or life-changing than Scripture. If it is drowned out in the noise of rhetorical gimmicks, emotionally charged flourishes, or frequent images and props, then the power in the message is diluted or even lost. At the same time, preachers are not simply verbal commentaries for our congregations. We are communicators. We need to connect with the audience. That is what preaching is. We need to recognize that the listener is not always ready to listen and that we need to get them there. Because the Bible is not boring, Bible-honoring preachers shouldn't be either. If we lean into the text of Scripture, we can teach it responsibly while commanding the listener's attention. We can preach sermons that are worthy of being heard.

CHAPTER 1

Preaching That Commands Attention

I first felt the pressure to preach sermons that "work" when I served at an inner-city mission ministering to at-risk teens in Chicago. Virtually every one of them struggled with fatherlessness, sexual abuse, and the pressures that come with rampant violence in their neighborhood. One thing about these kids—they had no poker faces. They lacked the decorum to look tuned in when they were not. They might talk to each other, stare at the ceiling, fall asleep—any number of clear signs that they were disengaged. The moment my preaching did not hold them, I could see it on their faces. From that time into the earliest days of my current pastorate, I sought to add to my sermon whatever I thought was needed to command attention.

I adopted an almost gimmicky approach. I didn't abandon expository preaching—I still preached the point of the passage and stayed with that passage throughout the sermon. But I thought I needed more than that. In essence, I was saying, "You're right, guys, the Bible is kind of boring. But I'll be such a dynamic speaker that you will learn to put up with the Scripture portions of my message and still be engaged. You'll walk away saying, 'That was good. That guy is good.'" Sadly, that is sometimes the feedback I received. That *I* was good. They enjoyed me. I learned how to get them to listen, so I assumed I was doing well, but I wasn't. It took some time before I realized what the problem was.

My problem wasn't that I wanted the attention of my listeners. It is right for a preacher to want to be heard. Of Jonathan Edwards's preaching, John Piper explains that he "could no more imagine speaking in a cold or casual or indifferent or flippant manner about the great things of God than he could imagine a father discussing coolly the collapse of a flaming house upon his children."[8] It is no badge of honor to preach boring sermons. Scripture is white-hot with the intent to rescue, to transform, and to change—how can we preach any portion of it in a cold, dutiful way? But if we *begin* with the desire to be heard, then we may clutter the sermon with elements that are meant to attract attention but actually serve to detract from the message. My problem wasn't that I wanted to command attention. My problem was the way I went about securing it.

THE TROUBLE WITH WINNING ATTENTION

Like me, you may have tried desperately to win attention in the wrong way. As I prepared sermons, I began to plug my outline full of attention-winning devices. I would literally lose sleep over this: "If I am not entertaining every few minutes or so, then I will lose them, and if I lose them they won't know this text." This was not a conscious thought, but it was the idea that was driving me. My number one desire was for my listeners to

8. John Piper, *The Supremacy of God in Preaching* (Grand Rapids: Baker, 2015), 105.

understand God's word, but I also wanted them to listen! Both desires were noble, but my strategy for gaining attention was tiring and, ultimately, not as effective as it could have been. I could spend hours burning most of my creative gas coming up with one home-run analogy only to win their attention for a moment. I needed something better, and so did they.

Most of us have our favorite attention-grabbing devices that we tend to gravitate to over and over. We might wander up and down the aisles because we believe movement is key to engagement. We might use props, images, personal experiences, funny stories—anything to keep the audience from getting bored. This is why I spent so many late nights toiling over my next analogy—illustrations where I would draw a parallel between a life experience and a point from Scripture. This was my device of first choice. Over time, some came to expect these fresh analogies in every sermon. It became a "thing" in my preaching. Sometimes after church I would receive a compliment on how engaging the illustrations were. I remember feeling partly glad that my preaching was appreciated. I also remember feeling slightly conflicted. Was the passage the highlight of the sermon or was my analogy? Have they come to merely expect analogies from me? My attempts at gaining attention were becoming a distraction, not only for them, but for me as well.

Not only can we become slaves to rhetorical devices but we can become blind to their real effect. Winning attention is really not difficult, but clearly some methods are better than others. If I shake the pulpit angrily, most people will snap to attention. But what have I compromised? If I toss bits of candy into the audience, few would remain inattentive. But what am I communicating? These may seem like extreme examples, but it is common for speakers to gain attention through tactics that are irrelevant to the message. The trouble is not gaining attention;

it is getting the audience to place their attention on your *message* that is the challenge. Thus, for the preacher, the goal is not to win attention but to focus it on the import of the scriptural text. Someone may approach us afterward to encourage us by saying, "That was great! You had my attention the entire time." We must not be content with such compliments. If we ask what the passage was about and they only have a foggy sense of it, we have failed in our goal as preachers.

Another reason some methods are better than others is because many of the commonly used techniques are only momentary in effect. The typical examples used in communication textbooks do not gain attention that persists. We are taught to insert a humorous anecdote here or some startling statistics there. Maybe a bizarre fact or an intriguing quote. Some encourage variation in pitch, pace, and tone. All of these are good because they offer on-ramps for the listener's attention to your message—they are not necessarily gimmicky. But they usually do not prompt listeners to *adhere* very long in their attentiveness. This is because these examples promote a punctiliar approach to gaining attention—appearing in spots throughout instead of a stream.

The thinking goes like this: every five minutes or so the average person's attention dwindles and must be revived. Therefore, the speaker must insert a rhetorical device aimed at gaining attention (a joke, a prop, stepping away from the podium, and so forth). The speech or sermon is dotted with points of focused attention like this:

. . . .

So not only is it a challenge to think of ways to bring the attention of the audience to the actual message, but it also must be done every few minutes. As soon as you have your audience's attention and begin to move on with the actual content of the exposition, it begins declining until the next point of attention. This approach relies on gaining involuntary attention. Involuntary attention is easy to gain because it is passive. Anything can arrest it. A sudden sound or sudden silence. Motion, light, colors—this kind of attention is instinctive but only lasts a moment.

Voluntary attention, on the other hand, is attention that is intentionally given to the speaker by the listener. The listener makes an internal decision: "This is interesting; I'm going to listen to this." The attention that the audience lends involuntarily must be converted into sustained interest.[9] That is, involuntary attention only lasts for a moment, whereas voluntary attention is sustained by the listener.

What I am looking for as a communicator is a way to capture attention in a more durative sense. I don't want attention to come in spurts or like blips on a screen. I want to win attention early on and keep it so that it looks more like this:

To gain sustained engagement, we need to use one primary method for commanding attention that serves as a constant throughout the sermon, buttressing along the way the attention that was won at the outset.

I'm not saying we should completely abandon traditional ways of winning attention. We can still employ humor, anecdotes, and the like. In fact, it is good communication to vary the landscape in this way. But illustrations and quotes function best as moments of clarity rather than moments of attention-winning. In other words, if the illustration or quote truly helps the listener understand the point you are making, then you

9. William G. Hoffman, *Public Speaking for Business Men* (New York: McGraw-Hill Book Company, 1923), 109.

should use it. If it doesn't, it is simply a device for attention and you don't need it. The devices typically used for gaining *attention* should instead be used for the purposes of *exposition*. We ask, "How can I help them understand this difficult point?" or "What would really serve to drive this home in their hearts?" rather than, "What can I insert here to get them listening again?" The listener can be engaged continuously throughout the message, and humor and anecdotes can now be used solely to enhance the clarity of that message.

In the effort to communicate, we must work at preaching in a way that commands attention. A scattering of rhetorical devices across the sermon doesn't sustain attention for the whole sermon, but there is a way to command and sustain attention. This way, I believe, is not only more rhetorically effective, but more sharply focuses an audience's attention on the content of the exposition. The key to this approach is the built-in *anticipation* that is latent in every text of Scripture. We keep the listener's focus on the passage by unveiling the *tension* that the passage will resolve.

HOW TENSION WORKS

Tension is the suspense that is generated when someone discovers there is something of interest that will soon be revealed. The tension experienced by a sermon's audience is one of expectation and anticipation. This is not to say that the listener is necessarily made to feel tense. Tension is simply the desire for resolution.

If you receive a phone call from a friend who starts with, "Hey, I've got great news for you!," you're going to experience tension. If your friend delays even for a second or two, you will likely ask, "Well? What is it?!" There is tension in the ultrasound room when expecting parents are waiting to hear from the nurse whether they are looking at a boy or a girl on the monitor. Children feel tension when they see wrapped presents under the tree. They want to open them so bad. It's a good tension. It's a hopeful anticipation that something needed or desired is coming.

Expert orators have been capitalizing on this since the dawn of rhetorical philosophy. The renowned Greek rhetorician Isocrates understood how tension works even at the level of the sentence. In order to press the advantage of suspense as much as possible, Isocrates popularized the use of the periodic sentence. Richard Katula explains: "In a periodic sentence suspense is maintained through several members until the meaning of the sentence is completed at the point of climax."[10] This would be achieved by withholding the subject and verb until the end of the sentence. An example for a preacher might be: "While we were yet sinners, when we rejected God, indeed when we still grieved him, *Christ died* for us." There is, within the sentence, a kind of buildup to the climax that the subject and verb provide. For Isocrates (and the many that would follow his style, most notably Cicero), the periodic sentence was highly effective because the stacking of ideas develops expectancy in the audience that there will be a resolution in the end.[11]

If suspense can function in the unfolding of a sentence, it can work across an entire speech. Just as a sentence may provide a succession of ideas culminating in a now-weightier subject and verb in the end, so may a speech or sermon provide a succession of movements climaxing in a now-weightier resolution

10. Richard A. Katula, "The Origins of Rhetoric: Literacy and Democracy in Ancient Greece," in James J. Murphy, ed., *A Synoptic History of Classical Rhetoric* (Davis, CA: Hermagoras Press, 1983), 13.

11. Katula, "Origins of Rhetoric," 13.

in the end. If listeners can anticipate something coming, they will lend their attention.

Let's think about this from the listener's perspective for a moment. You are trying your best to pay attention to a sermon, but the preacher drones on and on with no end in sight. You want it to end because you really don't care where it is all going, if it is even going anywhere at all. It is just difficult to stay attuned. In their book *Effective Public Speaking*, Joe Ayres and Janice Miller point out one of the reasons we fail to pay attention to a speaker: our intentional decision to label the speech uninteresting.[12] At some point along the way, we decide we are not able or simply not going to follow. If someone is laborious to listen to, most of us will not have the energy to force our attention for a long period of time.

Ayres and Miller then share tips on how to become a better listener. One such tip is for you to essentially generate suspense on your own while the communicator is speaking. They offer the following advice: "Anticipate. As you listen, you can think about what the speaker is trying to accomplish. ... This is an excellent way to build your interest in what is being said. It's like putting together a mental puzzle; you try an arrangement and then see if the speaker confirms it."[13]

The encouragement is for listeners to create questions they want answered and then to hang in attentively to see if those questions are addressed. But how much easier would this be if the speaker makes it clear what those questions are and how they are progressing toward the answers? The speaker should present questions that he knows the audience will want

12. Joe Ayres and Janice Miller, *Effective Public Speaking* (Dubuque, IA: Wm C. Brown Company Publishers, 1983), 35.

13. Ayres and Miller, *Effective Public Speaking*, 36.

answered, or else present statements that naturally prompt the right questions in their minds. This creates a positive tension as they await the resolution to all of the unsettled questions. This makes the audience interested in what the speaker is sharing. Tension creates interest—it *commands attention*.

This is no secret among writers. Have you ever loved a novel only to find out that literary critics can't stand it? In his book *Narrative Suspense*, Eric Rabkin probes the mystery of why certain books are so popular when they are widely considered poorly written. He provides example after example of works that continue to be read broadly over the years but do not match any conventional standards of literary excellence. He observes that, while the literary quality may not be very good, the reading itself may still be found to be worthwhile for many readers. Why? "Interest," he argues. "I knew a boy in high school who would read anything that promised to be about trains; and he would read nothing else. There was no use telling him Rousseau's *Confessions* is a great book, or that it is a good book. When there is no interest, books will not get read."[14]

A reader moves through a book via interest. Even if the quality of the writing is poor, interest will keep the reader engaged. This interest is captured and held through *suspense*. Rabkin continues, "Of course, our written language is linear. And of course, then, it must present progressions. But [the reader] is into this progression because, having been interested by the title, he waits now to find out more. 'And then?' He waits. And he reads while he waits. This is suspense."[15]

---

14. Eric S. Rabkin, *Narrative Suspense* (Ann Arbor: University of Michigan Press, 1973), 3.

15. Rabkin, *Narrative Suspense*, 5–6.

A speech, a book, a film that ignores the importance of maintaining interest is not going to be heard, read, or watched, no matter its literary or visual quality. The key to engaging the listener, the reader, or the moviegoer is to generate tension that promises a resolution. We need to learn how to shape our sermons accordingly.

SHAPING THE SERMON FOR TENSION

Developing tension has everything to do with the way in which the contents are laid out. Every presentation takes some shape, whether the speaker or writer did it intentionally or not. And the way that the message is shaped determines how much the audience will lend their attention to it.

The highly influential literary theorist Kenneth Burke has contributed much to this idea. In his seminal work *Counter-Statement*, he deals with the nature of form as it pertains to the shape a piece of literature is given in order to capture the audience.[16] He describes form or shape in literature as "an arousing and fulfillment of desires. A work has form in so far as one part of it leads the reader to anticipate another part, to be gratified by the sequence."[17] In other words, the communicator strategically sequences the communication so that the audience desires to move from one portion of it to the next. Anticipation (suspense) is generated through the careful sequencing of form.

Burke understood that it is not enough to provide an audience with good content. *The form or shape in which that content is delivered determines their level of engagement.* Before God spoke order into this world, the whole earth was "without form and

---

16. For Burke, literature means "written or spoken words." Kenneth Burke, *Counter-Statement* (Chicago: University of Chicago Press, 1968 [1931]), 123.

17. Burke, *Counter-Statement*, 124.

void" (Gen 1:2). If we don't bring order to our work as preachers, our sermons will be the same—chaos begging for order and purpose.

To form a message that captures and maintains interest, we must think from the perspective of the audience. As I mentioned in the preface, some do this by trying to discover what needs the listeners are likely to feel are most relevant. But for the expository preacher, forming a message for interest is not about felt needs. It is prompting the right need. It is about shaping the message in such a way that we are able to effectively bring our listeners with us to focus on a need that we know they have. Even if they haven't felt the need prior to the sermon.

Burke calls this kind of strategic form "the psychology of the audience." He explains, "Form would be the psychology of the audience. ... Or, seen from another angle, form is the creation of an appetite in the mind of the auditor, and the adequate satisfying of that appetite."[18] Once listeners sense a need to listen, they will lean in with full attention. But they do not get the answer right away. They will experience the resolution over the course of the sermon. This happens because of the way the message is shaped. Thus, to maintain tension, it is not enough to ask a question in the introduction and then promise an answer in the end. Rather, the entire discourse is an unfolding—shaped so that the audience is being incrementally moved toward the final resolution.

---

18. Burke, *Counter-Statement*, 31. Notice that Burke is not saying that we are to discover the felt needs of the audience but rather that the effective speaker produces the appetite in the listener, convincing them that this is what they are hungry for and that they should tune in for the satisfaction of that appetite. This does not fit "felt-needs" preaching; it fits the preacher who already understands what the listener needs (the import of the biblical text) and who seeks to convince them of that truth.

You've got to get people hungry for what they are about to hear. Burke's analogy of "appetite" is a good one. Simon Vibert observes in his book *Excellence in Preaching*: "The engaging preacher makes the meal enticing and at the same time promises that it will be nourishing."[19] Hunger is not resolved in one bite. Think of a gourmet meal—it is served in sequence. The appetizer comes first, the dessert last. Once an appetite has been exposed by the preacher (a need that connects with the audience and is uncovered by the text), the sermon then follows a pattern that maintains that appetite, feeding it one bite at a time. No one is uninterested in a meal when hungry.

To structure a sermon for interest, we must think in terms of the forms or shapes that sermons take. To maintain the audience's attention, those patterns must capitalize on tension. We should be like the historian Barbara Tuchman, who hung a little sign over her typewriter with a simple note: "Will the Reader Turn the Page?"[20] We, too, should adopt a page-turning strategy.

This won't happen by accident. Without an intentional strategy for winning an audience's attention, Calvin Miller says, "the not-so-communicative communicator talks on alone in his universe of bodies whose minds have been snatched away."[21] The preacher must raise a need and move the audience along in a sequence that carefully and gradually resolves that need.

Even if they haven't thought about it in terms of structuring their sermons, Christian preachers are already familiar with this way of thinking. Kenneth Burke referred to the relationship between tension and tension reduction as *guilt* and

---

19. Simon Vibert, *Excellence in Preaching: Studying the Craft of Preachers* (Downers Grove, IL: InterVarsity Press, 2011), 81.

20. Calvin Miller, *The Empowered Communicator: 7 Keys to Unlocking an Audience* (Nashville: Broadman & Holman, 1994), 109.

21. Miller, *The Empowered Communicator*, 111.

redemption. David Jabusch and Stephen Littlejohn write, "The religious overtones of Burke's terminology remind us of traditional Christianity's emphasis on sin (tension) and grace, or forgiveness (tension reduction)."[22] Since all of Scripture supplies some grace that sinners need, then every sermon can find this movement from problem to resolution. Every sermon can raise tension and resolve it.

TENSION ENHANCES EXPOSITION

What is most attractive about using tension as a rhetorical strategy in preaching is that it does not pull us away from the task of exposition—it leans us into it. This is because every passage of Scripture has tension already built in. Every passage contains inherent movement. It generates anticipation. Our task is not *creating* tension for the sermon but rather *discovering* the tension already at work in the text. As I have been saying, expository preaching does not begin with the audience's felt needs, but every Scripture passage reveals a deep need.

In order to understand the purpose of preaching, we must understand the purpose of Scripture.[23] In 2 Timothy 4, Paul urges his protégé Timothy to preach, but not before he explains the purpose of Scripture in chapter 3. Paul is saying, "Here's what *Scripture* is for (3:14–17), so this is what *preaching* is for (4:1–2)." Timothy was placed in Ephesus to protect the believers there from the danger of false teaching. Paul taught Timothy that the only way to combat this danger was to preach Scripture. Teaching Scripture is how a church is protected and made

---

22. David M. Jabusch and Stephen W. Littlejohn, *Elements of Speech Communication*, 3rd ed. (San Diego: Collegiate Press, 1995), 112.

23. I am grateful to the work of Bryan Chapell in *Christ-Centered Preaching: Redeeming the Expository Sermon* (Grand Rapids: Baker, 2005) where I first picked this up years ago in one of my first seminary classes. See pages 49 and 269.

healthy because only Scripture can yield that profit. So Paul wrote: "All Scripture is breathed out by God and profitable for teaching, for reproof, for correction, and for training in righteousness, that the man of God may be complete, equipped for every good work" (2 Tim 3:16–17).

In what sense is Scripture "profitable"? This is key to understanding the tension inherent in Scripture passages. Paul's point is that the value of Scripture is seen in its profit, its effect—it *does* something for us. Scripture works toward a profit, a better scenario, a change. New Testament scholar William Hendriksen wrote that Scripture "is a very practical, yes an indispensable, instrument or tool."[24] Scripture is a tool. Just as a nail gun is not an end in itself but rather a means to the end of driving nails, Scripture is the perfect tool to accomplish a particular task. That is why this term "profitable" (*ophelimos* in Greek) can also be translated "useful" or "effective"—it "describes that which is valuable not for its own sake but for the service it gives to men and to God."[25] Scripture yields a "practical benefit" because it *does something* to us.[26] What it does is complete us.

Paul uses four terms to describe *how* Scripture brings about its profitable effect in a person: through teaching, reproof, correction, and training. Yet it is not the *how* but the *result* or the ultimate profit of Scripture that is the point of this passage.[27] The effect that is brought about in a person (Timothy in this case) is *completion*.

---

24. William Hendriksen, *Exposition of the Pastoral Epistles,* New Testament Commentary (Grand Rapids: Baker, 1957), 303.

25. Jerome D. Quinn and William C. Wacker, *The First and Second Letters to Timothy* (Grand Rapids: Eerdmans, 2000), 763.

26. Ibid.

27. Philip H. Towner, *The Letters to Timothy and Titus,* NICNT (Grand Rapids: Eerdmans, 2006), 591; I. Howard Marshall, *The Pastoral Epistles,* ICC (Edinburgh: T&T Clark, 1999), 793, 795.

You can lay it out like this:

> Scripture profits you.
> *How?*
> Through teaching, reproof, correction, and training.
> *For what purpose?*
> To complete you and equip you for every good work.

The believer must be *exertismenos*—finished, completed, put into full working order.[28] "Complete" and "equipped" are "the real purpose for which [the Scriptures] are to be used."[29] Scripture teaches, reproves, corrects, and trains, but none of those are the ultimate goal. Rather, those are four ways that Scripture accomplishes its real goal. The goal of Scripture is to "complete" what is lacking—to make the man of God "equipped" or proficient to do good work.

Think about what this means for us and for our listeners. Scripture prepares us to do our work as ministers of the gospel. We need to be made spiritually competent in order to promote spiritual competence in others. It works for the minister first, and then works in the congregation. Each believer, on this side of eternity, is yet incomplete. There is always room for teaching, for rebuke, for correction, and for training in righteousness. All of Scripture does this because all of Scripture is inspired. Therefore, for every text, there is some way in which I am ill-equipped and the text before me was inspired so that I am properly outfitted. That is how Scripture profits the believer.

This is where we find tension. The Christian does not have all that is necessary to meet the demands of living for God.

---

28. Marshall, *The Pastoral Epistles*, 796.

29. Raymond F. Collins, *1 & 2 Timothy and Titus: A Commentary* (Louisville: Westminster John Knox, 2002), 265.

Scripture brings believers to a point where they are enabled to meet the demands that God places on them.[30] All believers are deficient in some area. There is some good work for which they are not ready (problem). They must be completed and equipped (solution).

FROM PROBLEM TO SOLUTION

The tension in every passage is the movement from problem to solution. Sometimes the text reveals the need explicitly. Romans 12:1–2 plainly tells us that we need to be able to discern the will of God and that we cannot discern it if we are conformed to this world. I need transformation, and the text tells me so straightforwardly. Sometimes the need is revealed more implicitly, as with most narratives—but the need is there just the same. We read about God's response to Cain's rage and learn something we need to know about God. In this case, God does not demand worship simply because he likes it. Worship is good for us, and the alternative way can only lead to sin's mastery over us. I need to learn this about God and worship and sin. Without this knowledge I am seriously lacking. Every passage reveals a need.[31]

If tension is the listener's desire for resolution, then what the preacher is doing in a sermon is identifying what the biblical text indicates that resolution is. The preacher begins the sermon by convincing listeners that whether they have been consciously

---

30. George W. Knight III, *The Pastoral Epistles,* 450; "able to meet all demands" W. Bauer, F. W. Danker, W. F. Arndt, and F. W. Gingrich, *Greek-English Lexicon of the New Testament and Other Early Christian Literature,* 3rd ed. (Chicago: University of Chicago Press, 2000), 136.

31. Bryan Chapell has called this the Fallen Condition Focus (FCF) of every text. The FCF is "the mutual human condition that contemporary believers share with those to or about whom the text was written that requires the grace of the passage for God's people to glorify and enjoy him." *Christ-Centered Preaching,* 2nd ed. (Grand Rapids: Baker Academic, 2005), 50.

aware of it or not, they have this particular burning need. The exposition confirms that need and how it can only be met in God's provision of grace. The sermon may teach us or train us where we are lacking in understanding. It may rebuke us or correct us where we are lacking in obedience. It will exhort us toward right thinking or right behavior from a place of wrong thinking or wrong behavior. The expository preacher's task is to discover how the passage accomplishes this. The preacher discovers what the text is trying to do. The audience receives an explanation of what the text says, and *why* it says it—why the text exists. There is a reason this particular truth is being revealed to us. It resolves something for us. Tension is built in to every passage because every passage addresses a particular need in a particular way. This is how preaching profits the hearer.

CONCLUSION

My problem early on in my preaching was not that I forsook the text. My problem was that I wanted to adorn the text with attention-commanding elements. Those elements often became the star, distracting attention from the text. When I learned to use the tension within the text itself, it was all the leverage I needed to keep listeners with me. Casting off the heavy burden of constantly chasing down the perfect analogy or the tightly matching illustration was a great relief. And the text became the star.

After this realization, my sermons became more biblically responsible because tension deals with resolution and this is how Scripture works. Since 2 Timothy 3:16–17 demonstrates that every passage of Scripture serves to profit each of us who is in some way deficient, every expository sermon should have tension and resolution. If the sermon does not bring to the forefront some sense in which the passage serves to equip the listener, it is a failed sermon. What other function should a sermon have but to render the profit for which Scripture was inspired?

Preaching with tension is also biblically responsible because thinking strategically about rhetoric is wise. Paul was not completely rejecting rhetoric or persuasion in 1 Corinthians 1:17 and 2:1–5. Rather, he was portraying the preacher as a conduit for the Holy Spirit's power as opposed to a purveyor of rhetorical ingenuity. We don't know just how much thought Paul put into his preaching strategy, but it is clear that he was diligent in seeking to persuade.[32] We should seek to persuade as well and, since persuasion is the very goal of rhetoric, we should adopt a rhetorical strategy that does not rob the gospel of its power—a strategy that is intentional and persuasive but does not overshadow Scripture's agenda.

We don't need to become slaves to gimmicks and ploys. In order to win the attention of listeners and keep it focused on Scripture throughout the sermon, preachers should employ the text's tension as their main strategy. Every sermon should make clear there is some problem or deficiency or confusion that we have, and the purpose of any biblical passage is to teach us, reprove us, correct us, or train us.[33] Tension is exposing this need and unfolding the solution. To command attention throughout the sermon, the preacher should think strategically about how to develop the sermon in a way that capitalizes on the inherent tension in the text.

---

32. See, for example, Acts 18:4 and 2 Corinthians 5:11.

33. This does not amount to every sermon functioning as a rebuke. Sometimes we are discouraged (problem) and we need to be encouraged (solution). We are often forgetful of wonderful truths about God (problem) and we need joyful reminders (solution). We may be largely ignorant of a profound truth (problem) and we need to simply learn it (solution). Examples abound but tension-shaped sermons should not be monotone. They should reflect the varied tones and textures of the Scripture passages they explain.

Structuring a sermon in a way that commands attention is going to take work. But if you are committed to expositing the biblical text and you want to preach in an attention-commanding way, I trust you will be helped by what follows.

CHAPTER 2

Discover the Problem-Solution

How would you feel if you faithfully followed your doctor's orders for years in the attempt to curb or reverse an illness only to find out you were misdiagnosed? According to one study, approximately twelve million Americans are given solutions to the wrong problem each year.[34] In a different but related study, it was determined that some of the most common causes include problems with ordering diagnostic tests, the lack of accuracy in patients providing their own medical history, and doctors misinterpreting, often rushing through, the test results.[35] It might be startling to think that 5 percent of patients in the United States come to the experts only to get misdiagnosed. But it seems to me that in churches across this land, the problem of misdiagnosis affects a much, much larger percentage of people. The causes are similar: diagnostic tests are not taken seriously, far too much weight is given to what the patients say about their

---

34. Jessica Firger, "12 Million Americans Misdiagnosed Each Year," *CBS News* (April 17, 2014), https://www.cbsnews.com/news/12-million-americans-misdiagnosed-each-year-study-says/.

35. Ibid.

own health, and the supposed experts are mishandling the test reports.

In our case, Scripture is the diagnostic tool and it contains all the health reports on humanity we need—the results are universal. But to nail the diagnosis, preachers need to not rush the study of the text. We need to prioritize the text over anecdotal information about the audience and handle the interpretation of the text responsibly. Let Scripture provide its own diagnosis and, within it, God has already provided his prescription.

In every sermon you must be clear on what the problem is so you can be clear about what the solution is. Together these comprise the principal purpose of the text. Every movement in the sermon will point to this one central problem-solution. The approach here is not to simply take a verse, explain it, and illustrate it, then rinse and repeat with the next verse. We are looking at the passage as a unit. We are unpacking how every piece of it drives the one overall agenda—the grace we need for a particular lack we have.

This problem-solution, distilled into one statement, is the thesis of your text. You were taught to write this way in your earliest English composition classes, where your teacher would tell you to discard everything in your essay that did not support your thesis statement. No matter how good it is, superfluous material would best fit another essay, not the one at hand. Articulating the main idea of the sermon is where the study of the passage reaches its pinnacle and the process of outlining the sermon can begin. When we approach a biblical text in our study, we must ask: "What is the big idea of this passage?" The answer is your thesis statement.

For those unaccustomed to this approach, it will prove challenging at first. For others, "big idea" preaching will sound familiar.[36] What must not be missed is that a sermon's thesis should not come from a personal arsenal of topics or favorite subjects. It should come from the passage of Scripture the preacher is committed to expound. Your task is to see in your exegetical work the primary truth that all of the passage is communicating. You then capture that truth in one concise statement so that your listeners get a unified sense of the whole passage. When we preach like this, we won't miss the diagnosis and appropriate prescription. And our listeners won't either.

TENSION IN THE HEART OF THE PASSAGE

Our task in Bible interpretation is to discover the agenda of the text rather than foisting our own upon it. We seek to discover the main idea, the heart of the passage. "But," you might ask, "does every passage really only have one main idea? Aren't there several ideas that can be mined from any one passage? If two preachers deliver sermons from the same passage but their main ideas are different, has one of them necessarily got the passage wrong?" Some may also wonder if preaching one main idea is really an effective communication approach. "Wouldn't that amount to sermons that are either too short or too repetitive?" These kinds of questions reveal the typical assumptions behind why many preachers do not hone the sermon down to one main point. But at the heart of every passage there is a primary truth given to profit us, and to miss that truth is to miss the mark in preaching. What's more, tension will be difficult to maintain without it.

---

36. Haddon Robinson, *Biblical Preaching: The Development and Delivery of Expository Sermons*, 2nd ed. (Grand Rapids: Baker Academic, 2001), 66.

Preachers should aim to communicate the tension in the heart of a passage for at least three reasons:

1. *Keeping to the tension inherent in every passage honors the text.* Expository preachers want to honor the text, and we can't if we don't understand the problem-solution at its heart. We are not to stuff the passage with our own ideas. Nor are we to find whole sermons in the weight of every verb or partial phrase. We are to go after what all the exegetical and contextual evidence points to as the communicative agenda of the text *and preach that*. No other reason stands on par with this one.[37]

2. *Keeping to the tension inherent in every passage is smart rhetorically*. It makes a sermon easier to listen to. As has been stated, listeners will find slightly related or wholly unrelated thoughts difficult to follow. But not only is a multidirectional sermon hard to track, it's difficult to ingest. What will your people remember about the passage after a sermon of thirteen points? Will they recall every point? Which should they remember most? If someone asked the average listener for the gist of a multiple-idea sermon, would they be able to communicate it? Adhering to one thesis statement that captures

---

37. There are two main ways preachers force ideas into a text. The first is the battering ram. This is to introduce ideas that are completely foreign to the text. These preachers mention the verse but never really dive in. They talk about their own thoughts and do not anchor them to the text—how can they when there is no connection? The other way is the Trojan horse. These preachers take a word or phrase in the text as their way in. But once they're in, it is evident that they have introduced ideas that do not flow logically from the text. What both of these methods have in common is the desire to use the Bible passage to promote the *preacher's* ideas rather than to analyze the text and discover *its* idea.

the text's heart enhances the effectiveness of communication.

3. *Keeping to the tension inherent in every passage generates anticipation in the best way*. As we will see, tension works best when there is one main dilemma and one main point of resolution. If preachers present several problems and promise several solutions, not only will they likely have left the intent of the text behind but they will have left the attention of most listeners behind as well.

In the first part of this chapter, I will unpack these three reasons in order to show you the importance of structuring your sermon so it gets its tension from the central idea of a text. Then, in the second part of this chapter, I'll discuss how to find the problem-solution in a passage.

KEEP TO THE TENSION INHERENT IN EVERY PASSAGE TO HONOR THE TEXT

Discovering and advancing the central truth of a passage is the duty of the expository preacher. This of course assumes that every passage communicates one central truth. This is debated widely and certainly merits more discussion than this chapter will allow. But for the preacher who holds to a high view of Scripture and who understands the basic function of literary communication, this should not come as a surprise.[38] Every passage seeks to convey one *primary* proposition. Certainly, a

38. There are many who believe it is the reader who brings meaning to the text. In that case, it is not that a passage of Scripture has multiple meanings, it is that it has no inherent meaning at all. For arguments as to why the Bible has meaning it is seeking to communicate rather than receptively absorbing whatever meaning the reader brings to it, *Is There a Meaning in This Text?* by Kevin Vanhoozer is an excellent resource (Grand Rapids: Zondervan, 1998). See also

Bible passage may present more than just one truth proposition, but there is only one that is primary. That onyx stones were used for the priestly ephod in Exodus 25:7 is not an unimportant truth, but a sermon that presents that fact as the salient burden of the passage is surely far afield from where it should be.

We might be tempted to think that treating Scripture this narrowly would shortchange the audience by not giving them all the truths a passage has to offer. But this is to misunderstand what Scripture is doing. When we articulate a passage's truth in one statement, we are recognizing that the author has an agenda in the passage and we are communicating that. So each sermon based on a passage of Scripture offers up what the text presents as a universally life-altering truth. It's not about being narrow; it's about being accurate. A few clarifications should be made at this point.

First, to say that there is one meaning is not to say that it cannot be expressed in different ways. The Platonic ideal in terms of wording is not what we are after. In fact, it will help your sermon to find different ways to word the thesis statement of the passage. Take two examples from 1 Thessalonians 5:16–18 ("Rejoice always, pray without ceasing, give thanks in all circumstances; for this is the will of God in Christ Jesus for you"):

> *A: Constant joy is a command that can only be fulfilled in Jesus Christ.*

> *B: We cannot rejoice always unless we are in Christ Jesus.*

David Clark's chapter "Scripture and the Principle of Authority" in his book, *To Know and Love God* (Wheaton, IL: Crossway, 2003), 59–98.

These two statements are different, but they are not saying anything different. The first statement makes the imperative nature of the text explicit, whereas the second assumes it. One says "constant", the other says "always." When two statements differ in wording, the meaning can remain intact. It is when they differ in concept that there is a conflict.

Now someone might ask, "Can't a passage say more than one thing?" A passage can say many things, but it says all of those things to advance the agenda of the primary truth it conveys. Thus, the need for a second clarification: you can preach a subpoint of a text but still fail to capture its primary meaning.

To stay with the example above, let's imagine a preacher has this statement as the focus of the sermon:

God has a will for us in Christ Jesus.

Maybe the pastor has been barraged with questions like, "What is God's will for my life?" Or perhaps the preacher wants to stamp out a spirit of deism in the gathered listeners and is looking to use this verse to do so. Does 1 Thessalonians 5:18 teach that *God has a will for us in Christ Jesus*? Yes, of course it does. Would it be wrong to preach this idea from this text? It could be.

Here we have a case where the meaning of the thesis statement is not *wrong*. It is not untruthful, and it is found in the text. The problem is that it is not the meaning that the whole text communicates. And this is dangerous. We would not want our listeners to think that we are teaching this as the primary truth of the passage. God having a purposive will for everyone is not why 1 Thessalonians 5:18 exists. Teaching a subpoint as the main point does not do justice to the text. At the very least, the preacher should teach the broader, primary meaning of the text and then explain that they will now spend more time on a particular subtheme. Or perhaps this would be an appropriate time for a topical sermon where several texts are introduced that make a cumulative case for a biblical truth. But we never want to teach a subpoint of a passage in a way that makes our listeners think that it is the main point of the passage. It's not only dishonest, it teaches a poor hermeneutic. A mishandling of Scripture that gets you a right truth from the wrong text will eventually lead to an untruth from any text. Again, we don't want to *insert* the point of tension; we want to *discover* it in the text.

Preaching a truth that is not the primary proposition of a text comes with a dangerous undercurrent. It may seem manageable at first, but if we are not careful, we can be swept out to the dark waters of eisegesis where we introduce our own problem-solution into the passage. You may have dynamic tension in the sermon, but it's not the tension *in the text*. If the preacher wants to talk about the idea that God has a specific will for each person—whom to marry, where to live, and so forth—there will be trouble finding these ideas in these verses because they are not there. To honor the text, the preacher will have to explain that the "will" referred to here has to do with rejoicing, praying, and giving thanks. If the preacher wants to broaden the application, this will need to be done by introducing other texts to justify it. But if we miss the author's intent, exposition is lost.

This is not an easy task, but it is necessary because of the nature of Scripture. It is communicating a meaning, and our job is to to understand it before we convey it in our preaching. Sometimes the meaning is complicated. Sometimes the passage is structured in an intricate way. Even if it is a complex passage or a complex truth, there is one primary truth. Complexity of meaning does not equate to plurality of meaning.[39]

---

39. Kevin Vanhoozer helps when he explains that there is one unified meaning in any given passage of Scripture, but there is a layered, multifaceted complexity with regard to 1) the author's intentions, 2) layers within the text,

In *The Big Idea of Biblical Preaching*, Duane Litfin reminds us that "God chose to communicate his inscripturated revelation in the form of ordinary human language, [and] that communication of necessity will consist of organized units of discourse. Thus, to understand that revelation we must discern these units and discover the ideas they embody."[40] After all, the presence of a primary proposition is what makes a passage a passage or a section. A passage is a pericope—a thought-unit centering on a unifying idea. "This is in fact what renders them 'units.' In other words, it is precisely the presence of a central idea that provides each unit its 'unit-y,' its 'unit-ness' so to speak."[41] When you choose a passage, you are recognizing that there is an overall unity to that verse or passage.[42]

---

3) readers' contexts, and 4) reading methods (though not all methods are equal). *Is There a Meaning in This Text?*, 417–18.

40. Duane Litfin, "New Testament Challenges to Big Idea Preaching," in Keith Willhite and Scott M. Gibson, eds., *The Big Idea of Biblical Preaching: Connecting the Bible to People* (Grand Rapids: Baker, 1998), 55.

41. Ibid.

42. In his book *Preaching*, Timothy Keller argues that "the concept of a 'big idea' within the text is … a bit artificial" (New York: Viking, 2015), 250. He sees it as too reductionistic. His reasoning is that often it is difficult to determine the main idea of a book and, when that is the case, it is much harder to determine the main idea of a passage within that book. He also asserts that Scripture passages are rarely written along the lines of classical rhetoric with one central proposition. Thus, he concludes that we must be wary of "expository legalism," where there is only one accurate way to handle a passage in a sermon. One can always return to a passage and "see new things and hear new messages." While I agree with Keller that good sermons can and will sound different on the same passage, I want to be wary of an "expository liberalism" where one passage is seen to produce any number of thoughts. It is not a matter of determining one main idea for an entire book (though I would argue central themes are retrievable). Nor is it a matter of classical rhetoric. It is a matter of the nature of communication—that there is a meaning in the text. It is often multifaceted, yes. We will continue to discover new insights that broaden and deepen that meaning. We will discern further applications and implications. Yet while the meaning is significant in many ways, it is not perpetually morphing.

Interestingly, to make his case, Keller draws from *The Big Idea of Biblical Preaching*, where every contributor (including Litfin) promotes the "big idea"

My third and final clarification is that a passage cannot mean something different from one generation to another, or from one culture to another. Often our geographical, grammatical, and historical distance from the original context makes this task challenging, but the problem-solution that the passage communicates does not change. Of course, one generation or one culture may see the meaning in a deeper way. One may also understand the *import* of the text's meaning in a different way. That is, the one meaning may bear on one context in a way that it does not in another. But this is not a change in meaning; it is a change in application. Every passage contains one meaning but can bear significance in many ways. However, while a text may be applied in multiple ways, it cannot be applied in unlimited ways. The significance of any text is controlled by its meaning. While there is relativity with regard to a text's significance, there is one normative meaning that must produce that significance.

Preachers may produce different main ideas from the same text, and that may or may not be okay. If they differ in wording, that's fine. They may even differ at the level of application. Further still, sometimes they will differ at the level of accuracy, and we don't need to fear that. It is simply the nature of the interpretive task. A friend of mine has suggested that it's like

---

approach. Litfin lists some challenges with it, but he in no way sees it as artificial. Much of my personal drive to "nail" the central import of a text comes from sitting under Litfin's tutelage. But perhaps in the end Keller and "big idea" preachers are not so far apart. Keller likens a passage to a town with roads. "Some texts have a simple, single point, while others are a bit more complex, just as some towns have one broad main street and others have a couple of main arteries that weave their way through" (68). I would say yes to this. The town limits are defined by the "subject," and multiple main streets means there are multiple "complements" (more on this in the following pages of this chapter). In the end, Keller and I would both affirm the same primary duty of the preacher: "Know the main point of the author and spend time there" (68).

trying to hit a bull's-eye. Some preachers might draft a thesis statement that does not match the text's meaning at all. They completely miss the target. Others may capture a portion of the meaning—they are on the target but far from the bull's-eye. There have been times when I am preparing a sermon on a text I have preached long before. I go back to see how I expressed the main idea in that previous sermon, and I am surprised to find that it is rather different from the one I have come up with this time around. This doesn't mean I was necessarily wrong then or that I am way off now. It may just mean that one of them is closer to the bull's-eye than the other. I need to do the work of figuring out which is closer, or if a third expression would be closer still.

Preaching one point of tension may feel quite new to some preachers. Many of us are accustomed to preaching sermons with multiple points and we don't feel like we are failing to honor the text. Preaching multiple points is not necessarily bad and, as we will see, sometimes necessary. But the danger of a sermon with multiple points is that typically those points are presented as equal to each other in hermeneutical weight. Most passages do not present lists with items of equal value that must be expounded. Some do this, but most do not. When preaching the Decalogue from Exodus 20 for instance, one may set out to cover "Ten Laws That Summarize Christian Morality." This works because the text is an actual list. But multiple-point preachers often see a list in every text. Thus, every sermon consists of five reasons for this or six steps to that.

We don't want to put subpoints on par with major points. And we don't want to take things that are incidental to the text's agenda and present them as a major concern of the text. That Jesus fed the multitudes with fish as opposed to some other protein cannot possibly be ranked on equal footing with the nature of the disciples' faith as they witnessed the event unfold. Every detail of every text is important, but not every detail serves as the main meaning of the passage. We need to stick with the problem the text is addressing and the solution that it offers. It is tension we discover, not tension we devise.

Even details that are significant and merit attention in the sermon should not automatically be treated as separate points. When Jesus rebukes his disciples about their faith (or lack of it) in Mark 4, he does so after rebuking a stormy sea into silence. Rather than treating those two rebukes as separate points, they should be explained as both pointing to the main intention of the passage. One may point out how Jesus can calm seas, how he reigns over all creation, how he is powerful and sovereign. Then one may move onto another point about how the disciples were weak in their faith and how Jesus challenges them on this. But the preacher should demonstrate that these are not separate points but rather that they are one and the same point. Jesus is asleep in the boat during a deadly tempest, just like Jonah. But where Jonah asks to be cast into the sea to be judged by God, Jesus judges the sea because he is God. The calming of the storm demonstrates what the disciples failed to believe—that Jesus was more than a man. These are not separate points to be made, but rather different stops along the journey of exposition, both pointing us to the same truth. The point of tension centers on the true nature of this man named Jesus.

Our commitment as preachers should be to find the primary import of the passage—the problem-solution in the text. Then we represent this meaning with one clear statement that will serve as the controlling point of tension for the entire sermon. We do this because of the conviction that texts are not springboards for whatever ideas we can imagine. They communicate an idea. While we may express that idea in different words or apply it in various ways, there are not limitless ways to word it and there are not endless applications. We strive to make the point of our sermon match the primary point of the passage as much as we are able.[43]

But finding the problem-solution in the text is not only about handling the passage responsibly. It's also about handling the audience responsibly.

KEEP TO THE TENSION INHERENT IN EVERY PASSAGE FOR CLARITY AND MEMORABILITY

If we preach sermons with several ideas, we are likely missing the real import of the text—the tension that the text itself provides. But another reason for keeping to the central idea of a passage is that it is smart rhetorically. This is true for at least two reasons.

The first is *clarity*. We see this in everyday life. When I sit at a restaurant in front of a multipage menu with seemingly endless options, I feel inundated. By the time I get to the third or fourth page of entrees, I have already forgotten what was on the first page or two. I appreciate a simple menu with a few good choices because then I can wrap my mind around the options. Focus enhances clarity. It is hard to understand someone when they are attempting to say many things. It is much easier to understand what they are communicating when they are saying one

43. Gerald Hiestand has made the case that sometimes a subpoint in a text can be the main point in a sermon. While I would agree, I would hasten to add that when a preacher feels it is necessary to take an incidental truth or subpoint and make that the focus of the sermon, two obligations follow: first, the preacher should always inform the listeners what the main point of the passage is so that they can understand the subpoint in its appropriate context. Second, since that truth is not the point the biblical author is trying to make, the case must be made from piecing it together with other passages in order to establish the applicable truth. In that sense it will have somewhat of a topical sermon feel. Gerald Heistand, "The Main Point of a Passage Should Not Always Be the Main Point of Your Sermon," https://www.preachingtoday.com/skills/2018/april/main-point-of-passage-should-not-always-be-main-point-of.html.

thing. The more clutter we add, the more clarity we lose. And you cannot maintain a thread of tension in your sermon when there is no clarity as to what the point of tension is.

A focused thesis statement also increases its *memorability*. The more we try to say, the more difficult it is for any listener to retain what we say. But when we are communicating one idea, it is very difficult to miss the point. Imagine asking your child to go to the pantry and get you twelve items without writing anything down. They are likely to forget something. But if you ask them for one item twelve times, they may become annoyed with you but at least they know exactly what you asked for. When a sermon stresses one main idea at every turn the listener will be best positioned to grasp the meaning of a passage and remember it. The entire thesis statement doesn't have to be communicated in every paragraph of the sermon, but every paragraph should serve to explain it or lead to it.

Preachers have been taught to use a variety of tools like handouts and visual aids in order to enhance retention. The more ideas we put into our sermons, the more we need to lean on presentation tools to aid memory. We intuitively know that the more content we add, the harder it is for our listeners to catch it or retain it. Rather than streamlining our content, we use tools to assist them in staying with us as we move them through point after point after point. A more effective strategy is to focus the sermon on one primary proposition using suspenseful anticipation as the leverage that will hold their attention.

This can be a difficult concept to ingest for preachers who know no other model than to create outlines with multiple, equal-weight points. They might think that preaching one primary idea is akin to emphasizing one of many equally viable points in the text at the expense of all the others. It may seem arbitrary to choose one, and it may seem to devalue the "other points" in the text. But this is wrongheaded. The multiple-point preacher is taking various observations that are either explicit in or inferred from the text and making them all equal by enumerating them, numbering them, and sometimes even alliterating them. The "big idea" preacher is not going to ignore those observations (if they are truly there in the text), but he is going to mention them *in relation to* the main idea.

The multiple-point sermon looks something like this:

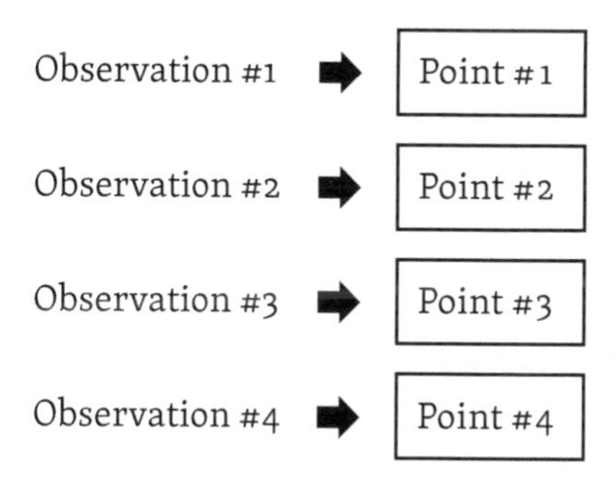

Again, some sermons will have to look similar to that—only when the Bible passage actually functions that way. But the preacher who is in the habit of overlaying this pattern on every text should consider breaking that habit.

The big idea sermon will most often look like this:

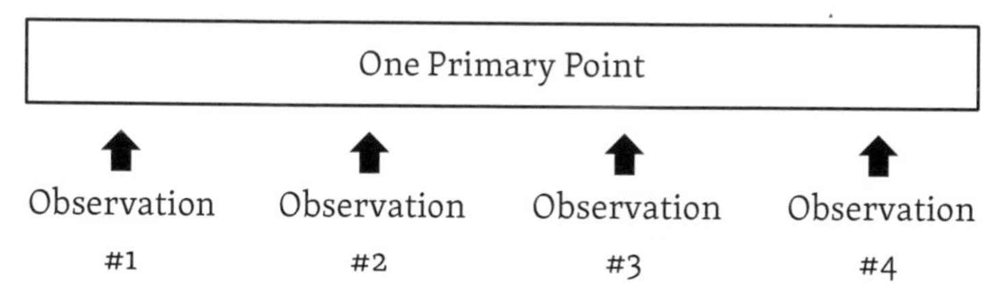

This is not about making only one primary application. It is not that the text can only be shown as relevant in one way. This is not even to say that the primary point only has one angle to it or that it can only be stated in one way. It is to say that there is one central idea the text communicates and we will use all our observations in the text to point to and drive home that meaning. Each observation does not simply end in repeating the primary point, but each observation develops the primary point.

In order to preach in an attention-commanding way, we need to communicate clearly and memorably. People in our audience need to be able to track with us easily—easily enough that after the sermon they could confidently repeat to a friend what the sermon was about. We work against this aim when we preach several ideas instead of one. We'll see this even more clearly when we look at how a singular train of thought best produces anticipation in the listener.

KEEP TO THE TENSION INHERENT IN EVERY PASSAGE TO GENERATE ANTICIPATION IN THE BEST WAY

Preaching the thesis of the text is crucial to preaching that commands attention. Not only is it demanded by the nature of responsible interpretation, and not only is it the best way to be clear and memorable, but it is the best way to generate anticipation in the listener. Tension in a sermon requires a "big idea" because tension requires a stated problem and expected solution. If a sermon offers to address a myriad of problems and promises a variety of solutions, tension will dissipate. All the pieces of a sermon, all the observations along the way, should point to and develop one central problem and expected solution. In this way, the preacher capitalizes on the listener's need for that solution throughout the entire sermon.

Great writers like Ernest Hemingway know this. *The Old Man and the Sea* is a story about an old man, Santiago, who was once a legendary fisherman but has now become a laughingstock. He has not had a catch in over eighty days. A young boy is the only person left who has any respect for him, but the boy's parents will not allow him to fish any longer with the tired, apparently cursed old man. In the book, Santiago goes out on a quest to get the catch of all catches—an undeniable trophy that could recapture his legendary status.

As you read that description, you likely see tension in the narrative. There is a problem and a struggle toward what we hope will be the resolution of that problem. That hope for resolution is why we lean in to read. We also identify with the old man. We are gripped by Santiago's story because it is in many ways like ours. None of us wants to feel insignificant; none of us wants to be overcome by old age and forgotten. None of us wants to be mercilessly burdened with sad longing for our yesterdays. We would rather plunge forward, face difficulties with courage, and aim for more glorious days ahead.

Now, Hemingway also includes many smaller details along the way. Some of them seem superfluous: Santiago's love for his baseball hero, Joe DiMaggio; his dreams of being a teenager again, watching young lions play on a beach in Africa; strange details about the physical torture he endured as he wrestled with a mighty marlin. But when you understand what Hemingway is doing, you realize these are not superfluous at all. Far from filler, they are details that help point the reader to the primary burden of the book: a man on a quest to recapture strength and prestige.

Joe DiMaggio is Santiago's hero even during a season when he is not playing well. He knows DiMaggio will rise to his former status again—he must, for Santiago sees himself in Joltin' Joe, and he has to believe he can once again be the fisherman he once was. Santiago's dream of young lions hearkens back to his days of strength and vitality. Lions represent power and unchallenged status in the animal kingdom. Santiago's wounds, and especially his verbal expression of pain, call to mind a man who's being pierced through by a nail making its way through his hands and into the wood. At the end of his journey, he must carry his mast across his lacerated back as he climbs toward his shack. After falling under the weight of the mast, he finally makes it to his bed, where he plops down in a cruciform position. These are not-so-subtle ways of presenting him as a sort of Christ figure in that he must reach his victory through humiliating pain and suffering.

It would not have made sense for Hemingway to reference a baseball player who was currently on a hot streak. It would not have worked to reference a dream where defenseless rabbits nestled in a den or to include echoes of Christ's birth rather than his suffering. Those would have been details that worked against the primary idea. Instead, all those important elements work to support the main idea.

If you were to give a report on this book, you wouldn't make it about five or six different subjects. Instead, you would center the essay on one thesis—perhaps something like "Great valor is found in the indomitable spirit." You would describe how the various elements in the novel point to and confirm that thesis. "Five ways to overcome hardship" would hardly cut it. The above elements do not stand alone as the thesis of the work, but they work together to demonstrate it. These little details contribute to the tension of the book. Those varied bits of information are indeed relevant and part of why the book won a Pulitzer Prize. The same principle applies to our preaching. We do not take every passage and look to break it down into several equally weighty points. Instead, we look to see how the author is using various details in order to drive home the primary idea. If the preacher sees the various details as loosely connected points, it will be difficult to carry tension because there is no cohesion. The details in the text push forward one main thought.

The various observations we make in the text are not isolated truths but form a unified whole. Tension works best when the preacher understands this principle.

This works even with nonnarrative portions of Scripture, and it works even at the level of a paragraph. Let's use Romans 13:11–14 as an example:

> Besides this you know the time, that the hour has come for you to wake from sleep. For salvation is nearer to us now than when we first believed. The night is far gone; the day is at hand. So then let us cast off the works of darkness and put on the armor of light. Let us walk properly as in the daytime, not in orgies and drunkenness, not in sexual immorality and sensuality, not in quarreling and jealousy. But put on the Lord Jesus Christ, and make no provision for the flesh, to gratify its desires.

We can state the central thought this way: *Because Christ's return is near, we must strive to live righteously.*[44] Every phrase, every sentence in that paragraph drives home that idea. Paul begins by establishing the reason for the action he wants his readers to take. Christ's return is drawing closer every day, so we should not be squandering our time. So then, what should be our focus? Living righteously. Paul describes this as two halves of the same action: we throw off darkness and put on light. What does that look like? It looks like the diligent stamping out of immoral behaviors. It is the refusal to gratify the desires that would prompt us to behave in those ways. But, honestly, does any one of us have the power to actually do that? Of course not. That's why he makes it clear that the only way to do this is to wear

44. This can be worded a number of different ways, but the basic components should be there.

Jesus like a garment—you have him as your source of strength. You are enveloped by him.

In the above example, it is easy to see how every portion of the paragraph matches the thesis statement. Each verse points to it, supports it, unpacks it. But suppose I made this into a three-point sermon?

When we understand Jesus' return is nearing, we will:
Wake up—stay alert to the fact that Christ is returning.
Cast off darkness—we need to eradicate sinful behaviors.
Put on Christ—Jesus must be our focus or we will fail.

The text is represented in each point, but as a whole the outline doesn't represent the text well. The congregation is made to understand the text as having three points when it really has one point. That Christ's return is nearing is the reason for the action of living like Christ. "Cast off" and "put on" are not separate points or sequential steps; they are one and the same. To do one is to do the other. And both are the appropriate response to the reality of Christ's coming return. This may seem like a subtle variation to some—a nitpicky criticism—but it makes a difference. Is Paul saying, "Here are three responses to the Lord's return?" No, he's not. He is saying we should live the right way because the Lord is returning. The one main idea of the text is muddled when I turn it into three points. Would we really want to communicate that the *first* response to Christ's return is to wake up, the *second* is to cast off sin, and *then*, after those are successfully accomplished on one's own, to put on Christ? Surely not.

Now, the tension-attuned preacher will make those three stops along the way. We have to explain the text in a linear progression—we can only explain one thing at a time. Yet we can move from one thought to the next without making each move a separate point, as if each were a step or separate action. Furthermore, I will lessen my ability to employ tension with three separate points about how to respond to Christ's return. This is because there is less flow between the portions of the text when I break them up that way. Santiago's dreams are not a separate point from his love of Joe DiMaggio. They both serve one and the same point. Casting off sin is not a separate point from putting on Christ. When we show people that the text is actually doing something or going somewhere singular, we can weave that thread of tension to keep them moving along with the text. We will still need to unpack the paragraph one piece at a time, so naturally we will talk about casting off sin before we talk about putting on Christ. But we don't need to do so by calling them "steps" or separate points. Rather, we can move through the text tying every piece to the one primary idea, not three ideas. We will see how this works when we look at how to outline sermons in chapter three.

Again, the preacher needs to focus on the main idea the text conveys and build on the tension inherent there. The sermon's thesis statement needs to be clear, succinct, and singular for tension to work well. But the preacher must also keep in mind that the "points" along the way should be sequenced to emphasize the main idea in an unfolding way. Otherwise tension is lost. Kenneth Burke reminds us that attention is sustained through the careful sequencing of the literature's form.[45] One part of the sequence must lead to the next. When a sermon consists of multiple propositions, it becomes extremely difficult to connect the ideas in a sequence where one leads to another in a suspenseful

45. Burke, *Counter-Statement*, 124.

way. In order to maximize tension, the preacher should focus on the primary thrust of the passage.

BREAKING DOWN THE BIG IDEA

At this point you might be wondering how a sermon thesis is determined or what it even looks like. If a singular statement is so crucial to harnessing the tension in a passage, we should understand what it is and how to create it. In *Biblical Preaching*, Haddon Robinson explains that every idea is composed of two parts: the subject and the complement. A subject without a complement is not a complete idea.[46] As Robinson would explain, the subject is what the preacher is talking about. A complement is what the preacher is *saying* about what he or she is talking about. Many have found it helpful to put it in terms of a question and answer, with the subject a question and the complement the answer. Essentially this is what a good thesis statement is. A question is proposed and answered. There is a problem and a solution.

For example, *obedience* alone cannot pass as a proper subject. It can serve as a grammatical subject but not the subject of a communicative idea—it's not enough. *Obeying your leaders* is a subject. It can be put into question form: *Why should we obey our leaders?* The complement would be the answer to the question: *We should obey our leaders because they watch over us*—this is a thesis statement. A thesis presents a topic and says something about that topic. It asks a question and answers it. It does not merely present a *what* or a *who* but also presents a *why* or a *when* or a *how*. This is important to understand, because without a complement it will be impossible to determine a need.

---

46. See Robinson, *Biblical Preaching*, 41–46.

Subject: We should obey our leaders. (Why?)
Complement: Because they watch over us.

When you consider what goes into determining how many verses you will be preaching from in the first place, you will see that this process already puts you on your way to discovering the thesis statement for your sermon.

DETERMINING YOUR PASSAGE LENGTH

When thinking about how to determine the thesis of a biblical passage, we need to begin by considering what constitutes a "passage." Our thesis examples so far have been from very short texts for the purpose of easy demonstration. But length is determined by what the biblical author is doing and how long it takes the author to do it. You are looking for a unit of thought or a *pericope* (taken from the Greek meaning "section"). You won't want to simply snip Scripture here and there to create any length of passage you desire. You want to discover the agenda in the text and divide the preaching units accordingly. You're looking for the tension point—the subject and complement, the question and answer, the problem and solution. Sometimes it might be as small as a paragraph. It could be even smaller—for instance, if you have a proverb that seems to stand alone. It could be hard to squeeze an entire sermon out of one verse and remain faithful to good exegesis, but you might supplement it with other verses in the Bible to fill it out. But normally you will deal with a paragraph or series of paragraphs that all seem to make one point—they communicate one thesis. They center on a singular problem-solution truth.[47]

---

47. See Appendix B, "Sample Map of a Sermon Series on Exodus," for examples of how I divided passages over a series.

Three guidelines will help when selecting a passage and determining its length. Approaching each text like this will put you well on your way to determining the text's thesis, your "big idea."

LOOK FOR PATTERNS THAT HELP DEMARCATE UNITS THAT THE AUTHOR INTENDED

Let's say you are preaching through the book of Judges. You might initially decide you want to preach one sermon for each of the judges—the leaders God raised up to deliver Israel throughout the book. This would give you twelve if you combine Deborah and Barak in Judges 4–5 and do not count Abimelech as a judge. But as you map out your sermon series, you may realize that some of them don't give you much to work with for a sermon. Shamgar, for instance, gets one verse (3:31). Not a lot of detail there. Nor will that text produce much that is different from some of the other judges' stories.

As you study, you begin to realize that the author probably did not intend each judge to constitute a literary unit. This is not merely because some are given more real estate on paper than others, but because there is another pattern that becomes apparent upon further scrutiny. It turns out that when you look for literary patterns, you see that Judges can be broken down into six clear cycles.[48] Each cycle covers a period of Israel's wayward turn from Yahweh, their consequent oppression by neighboring rulers, their cry of suffering, and God's raising up a judge to deliver them. You can preach an initial sermon on the prologue before the cycles begin, and perhaps you finish the series with a sermon on the final chapters' post-cycles look

48. Daniel I. Block, *Judges, Ruth,* New American Commentary (Nashville: Broadman & Holman, 1999), 73.

at the moral plight of Israel. If you are willing to treat some of the longer cycles (like Samson's) in one sermon, you would have at least eight preaching units—an eight-part sermon series. Each of these would have its own thesis. These are different enough from each other that the author decided to spend time unpacking them at length and with peculiar details. They each have their own point of tension the author is developing differently.

Identifying theses and passage lengths has much to do with your "zoom" level. Sometimes you will see an author moving more quickly through episodes to make a larger point, and so you might zoom out a little in order to reflect that agenda. If you are preaching through Mark, you could preach Jesus' baptism and temptation separately—a sermon each. Or you could zoom out, seeing that Mark is moving quickly, and see a larger thesis that is served by both events. You could preach both paragraphs together seeing how they both support a larger thesis. You could zoom out another level and encompass John the Baptizer's ministry and how it sets up Jesus' baptism, temptation, and proclamation of the gospel. It would not be wrong to zoom all the way out and preach the Gospel of Mark in one sermon. You could do the same with Judges or any book. You would identify the overarching thesis of the entire book and then walk the audience through select passages to showcase how the author is delivering that message in that book.

It is important to determine passage lengths with an eye to commanding attention in the sermon. You will not want to simply turn to the outline provided in the first few pages of your favorite commentary and make your sermon series based on the major points there. Some units will need to be combined, and some thesis statements will need to be more finely tuned. We will deal first with the former.

Unless you are preaching the thesis of the whole book in one sermon, you are breaking it down into a succession of sermons and you will not want one sermon to sound exactly the same as the previous one or a recent one. There will be times where you seem to have two back-to-back units that produce much the same thesis. There may be other reasons you initially divided them into separate literary units, but if they both support the same thesis, combine the units. Preach the one thesis with two passages rather than in two sermons. You will have a hard time keeping your listeners if they essentially hear you saying, "Last week we looked at this idea, and this week we're going to see the same idea and same implications but from the next few verses." If successive sections in Scripture communicate the same basic thesis, consider preaching them together even if you can't cover every exegetical detail in each verse.

Other times, when the passages with nearly identical theses are located several units from each other, it might be hard to combine them. So you follow the next guideline.

WHEN PREACHING A SERIES THROUGH A BOOK, BE CAREFUL TO FINE-TUNE YOUR THESIS STATEMENTS TO MATCH THE UNIQUE VOICE OF EACH UNIT

This should be the commitment of every expositor who believes that all Scripture is inspired and profitable. But there is a practical attention-related concern as well. It will be difficult for your listeners to lean in and stay attuned when they feel like they have heard your sermon already. There's no tension in any question to which we feel we already know the answer. Returning to the example from Judges, let's say you decided you are going to divide the book into a prologue, six cycles, and a final outlook on Israel's condition. Each of your cycles promotes essentially the same broad thesis; something like, "*When we are mired in sin and its consequences, we can cry out to God who alone can deliver us."* This basic thesis does not really change from one unit to the next. But that doesn't mean each cycle is not worthy of its own attention (otherwise the author would not have written it). So we must determine how *this* particular passage delivers the overall thesis in its own unique way. We're narrowing our way down to the passage's subject—the problem it is addressing.

Some of the key questions you will want to ask include:

- What does this passage reveal to us about God?
- What does this passage reveal to us about ourselves and how we should respond to God?
- How does this passage *in particular* drive these truths home to the reader?
- If this passage did not exist, what profit would we be missing?

The Deborah/Barak cycle and the Gideon cycle each drive home the same general truth about rebellion, despair, and deliverance. But one deals with Barak's unwillingness by employing the determination of Deborah to goad him. The other deals with Gideon's lack of trust. God stoops to Gideon's little faith by demonstrating to him again and again that he is to be trusted. You can tease these out in your thesis statements so that they bear the unique voice of their respective passages. Your sermons will not sound the same because you are proclaiming the passage's specific take on the general, repeated thesis.

When determining your passage length, you may decide that some units are too long for one sermon to manage. Or you may decide that a longer unit is worthy of your taking more than one sermon to work through it in your context. In this scenario, you will need the third guideline.

IF A UNIT SEEMS TOO LONG TO PREACH, YOU MAY BREAK IT DOWN INTO SUBUNITS—CAREFULLY

You can take longer sections and break them into smaller preaching units but you must do so cautiously. The Samson cycle, for example, is four chapters long (Judg 13–16). Preachers should develop the competency to handle long sections in one sermon, but you don't always have to. You can choose to zoom in a little more. If you decide to preach a unit in multiple sermons, you will want to take precautions so that you do not hijack the author's agenda at any point. If pericopes across an entire book can share the same basic thesis, so much more will units within a section share the same communicative goal. When you are determining the unique voice of each subunit in Samson's cycle, you will want to see how they differ from one another, but the thesis should not be alien to the overarching program of the larger section. You need to be sure there is enough textual evidence to support the thesis you are seeing. You are looking for a tension in a shorter section that belongs to a broader theme of tension in the larger section.

Let's take a subunit within Samson's cycle. The lines can be drawn differently depending on your "zoom level," but for our purposes here I will take the first episode in the story of Samson and the Timnite woman (Judg 14:1–20). Take a moment now to familiarize yourself with that chapter. If you were teaching a preaching class and asked your students to submit what they think the thesis of this passage is, you may receive a wide array of suggestions. When you are determining the thesis of a passage, you will be vetting options in your head like a professor would assess student theses.

Some you will immediately dismiss as erroneous. Suppose a student postulates that Judges 14:1–20 teaches: *We should never introduce a difficult riddle at a wedding because it will lead to disaster.* This would probably strike you immediately as problematic. What is this passage revealing to us about God—his displeasure toward difficult riddles? What's it saying about us and how we should respond to God—when and where to use riddles? How to behave at weddings? Is it universally true that riddles at weddings will lead to disaster? More importantly, is the text communicating that what led to disaster was the use of a riddle? Not so much. This thesis gets the uniqueness down, but it leaves the author's agenda behind.

Further investigation will get you closer. Perhaps the thesis is more in the vicinity of this statement: *When we allow a hot temper to go unchecked, we will suffer disastrous consequences.* After all, the text does inform us that "hot anger" was a motivation for Samson (14:20). He does seem angry toward his parents in the opening few verses. Surely this episode speaks to disastrous consequences, and this complement will likely make it into our final version of the thesis. But the part about temper does not hold up to the questions we always ask about a passage when we are looking for a thesis. It's not that the passage has nothing to say about anger; it's that we are looking for something that reflects more of the evidence than just a brief mention. The text does not seem to emphasize anger as its *primary* burden. It matters but it is not the star of the show. We can keep it as an option, but further study will likely lead us to see that the nasty temper was part of a bigger problem.

We need to take our cues from the author more diligently. In the first three verses, "Timnah" is referenced three times and "Philistines" is also mentioned three times. That's quite repetitive for three verses. Why the repetition? Is Samson supposed to marry a woman from among the Philistines? Absolutely not. He tells his parents he wants to marry a Timnite woman. They object. He demands it because it is right in his own eyes. Their eyes (and the Lord's) do not matter to him. Thus, he dishonors the Lord and his parents. Is this important to the author? "Father and mother" is written six times throughout this chapter, and "father" alone another three times. Exegesis involves more than simply counting how many times words are repeated, but in this case, it is hard to ignore. It is clear that Samson breaks God's explicit commands—the Israelites were to drive *out* the nations, not marry them (Deut 7:1–5)! He also breaks the fifth commandment of the Decalogue by egregiously dishonoring his parents (Exod 20:12). He speaks to them with demands and then defiles them by serving them honey taken from a lion carcass without telling them (Judg 14:9). Samson is supposed to live differently than the Philistines and deliver Israel from them, yet he lives in the opposite direction. Ironically, he reaps disastrous consequences for himself while he winds up accomplishing God's purpose for him anyway (vv. 4, 19). Samson is angry, sure. He's miserable. God has blessed him unimaginably but he's ruining himself, his family, and his people by doing what is right in his own eyes instead of God's.

So each cycle in Judges bears the same basic message: *When we are mired in sin and its consequences, we can cry out to God, who alone can deliver us.* But Samson's cycle can be more fine-tuned: *When we presume upon God's grace, we lead lives of destructive disobedience that will make us miserable.* That is more specific to Samson's story. But if we're taking just 14:1–20, we have to get more specific yet: *When we delight in our own morality instead of God's laws, we suffer unnecessary consequences.* When you get to the episode about Delilah, you will need to recognize the parallels with the story about the Timnite woman. But your thesis will need to be specific to the Delilah episode. It might look this: *When self-reliance replaces obedience, disaster ensues.* E of these is true in life, matches the rest of Scripture's teaching, and fits under the banner of the overall agenda in the book of Judges, and yet they all hold true to the unique voice of the unit they represent. As closely related as they are, they are distinct enough to create tension in each sermon based on their individual take on the broader thesis.

DETERMINING YOUR SERMON THESIS

Determining your textual unit puts you well on your way to discovering the unit's thesis. By this point you will already have a good sense of it, and now it is time to articulate it and sharpen it. The questions you have been asking of the text give you at least a broad sense of what is going on in the passage. You should already have at least a sentence or two written down that represent the gist of the text. Now you'll want to get more specific in order to articulate a one-sentence thesis for your sermon. At this point, you will need clear answers to the following questions:

- What problem or question is the passage solving or answering? What issue is it addressing? (You are looking for the *subject*.)
- What solution or answer does the passage offer with regard to the primary issue it is addressing? (You are looking for the *complement*.)

Once you have the subject and the complement, there will often be one more level of honing that needs to take place. When you first articulate your thesis, it may be stuck in time, making it difficult to make sense of for today's audiences. If you studied Judges 14:1–20, you may have come up with something like,

Samson delighted in his own morality instead of God's laws, so he suffered loss and became violent. That would be true to the text. But the purpose of preaching is to bring the text to bear on the people before you. That's interesting for Samson, but how does this speak to your people today? So we can say "you" instead of "Samson" *if* what was true for Samson then is true for us today. A better option than "you" might be to use "we," since the preacher is not excluded from the weight of the truth. We tend to delight in our own sense of right and wrong and, though we may not live under Nazarite restrictions, Samson broke more laws than just those. So we can say "God's laws" in general, and that works for today's audience too—God reveals dos and don'ts, but we prefer to create our own where we see fit. Samson suffered loss (the bride he wanted, his best man who married her, and debt for losing the riddle game) and he became murderous in order to pay his debt. Does that happen to us today? That's pretty specific. Scripture does not bear out that every disobedience will lead to those particular consequences. But while we may not suffer those *specific* consequences, we do suffer from disobedience in general. God's laws are given for a reason, and when we stray from his guidance, we are not making our lives better. God accomplishes his purposes anyway, but we lose in disobedience. This bolsters the overall point of the whole book of Judges. Thus, we can hone the thesis to read more universally: *When we delight in our own morality instead of God's laws, we suffer unnecessary consequences.*

To close the chapter, let's look at two further examples where we will quickly move from investigation of the text to the articulation of the "big idea." First, we will turn to Psalm 100—it's five verses long and will not take much time to read carefully.

PSALM 100

Make a joyful noise to the LORD, all the earth!
Serve the LORD with gladness!
Come into his presence with singing!

Know that the LORD, he is God!
It is he who made us, and we are his;
we are his people, and the sheep of his pasture.

Enter his gates with thanksgiving,
and his courts with praise!
Give thanks to him; bless his name!

For the LORD is good;
his steadfast love endures forever,
and his faithfulness to all generations.

When we begin by asking what this passage reveals to us about God and what kind of response it seeks from its readers, we see that it has something to do with God's goodness and how he is worthy to be praised. We also ask how this psalm in particular drives home its idea, so we look at the particulars.

Working through our questions as we study, we come up with something like the following:

- ***What does this passage reveal to us about God?*** That he is worthy to be praised.

- ***What does this passage reveal to us about ourselves and how we should respond to God?*** That we should make a joyful noise in our serving and singing to him. That our praise should be glad and thankful.

- ***How does this passage in particular drive these truths home to the reader?*** The psalmist demands a certain kind of praise—it should be joyful, glad, thankful. It should express itself in singing. The psalmist also provides grounds for such joyful singing, namely, the nature of our belonging to God and the goodness of God.

- ***If this passage did not exist, what profit would we be missing?*** Various psalms invite the Lord's people to sing. Various psalms provide reasons why God is worthy of it. But let's take one particular feature: the phrase "sheep of his pasture." This is not the only instance of the phrase in the psalms. There are three other psalms that use it, but each of them carries with it a "negative" theme. Psalm 74 uses the phrase in the first verse to make the case to God that he should intervene on their behalf in the midst of their oppression. "How long, O God, is the foe to scoff?" (v. 10). Similarly, Psalm 79 contains twelve verses pleading with God for judgment on the defiling nations. Then it ends with the thirteenth verse stating that, as the sheep of his pasture, they will thank God forever. Finally, Psalm 95 also contains the phrase but immediately follows it with a warning not to harden one's heart on hearing God's voice (v. 7). What stands out with Psalm 100 is that there are no pleas for God to judge oppressors and there is no warning against rebellion. It maintains a thoroughly positive perspective throughout. The thesis statement, then, should carry a positive ring to it rather than warning or desperation.

- ***What problem or question is the passage solving or answering? What issue is it addressing?* (You are looking for the *subject*.)** The subject might be expressed this way: *We should worship the Lord with enthusiasm*. The "should" language is not negative, but it expresses the imperatival nature of the opening verses. We are being prompted, invoked. "Worship" is an attempt to capture singing, serving, entering with praise and giving thanks. This is what we are being called to do. "Enthusiasm" further defines that call—our worship should be joyful and glad.

- ***What solution or answer does the passage offer with regard to the primary issue it is addressing?* (You are looking for the *complement*.)** The complement can be put this way: because he is a Good Shepherd. The "because" is the transitional word being that the complement is a reason to worship God. The reasons are given to us in verse 3 (because he is our creator and we are his sheep) and in verse 5 (because he is good and his love endures forever to all generations).

  At this point you will want to ask whether these are separate complements or can be stated as one. Again, it would be easy to turn this into a multiple-complement sermon. We could say that first he is our Creator; second, we are his sheep; third, he is good; and so on. But in this case, I am not sure the psalmist is giving numerous reasons, but rather aspects of one reason. This is debatable, and you have to make your call. I would go with

> one complement that encompasses verses 3 and 5. It seems to me that verse 3 is getting at his ownership over us (by virtue of his making us) and that the sheep/shepherd relationship is the dominant metaphor. Verse 5 explains that he is a certain kind of shepherd just as he deserves a certain *kind* of worship. He is good. That he is loving and faithful further defines that goodness. Thus, *because he is a Good Shepherd* will work as the complement. The sermon will unpack the details.

The unit was easy to determine, since psalms are units themselves. It is not so long that we needed to wrestle with breaking it down further or zooming in. And the thesis is not too wordy, yet captures the problem-solution of the psalm well. The problem raised is our need to worship enthusiastically. It is an issue worthy of being addressed because we fail to understand why we should worship with gladness. The complement is the way in which the psalm resolves the issue—it gives us a reason. So to state it in question and answer form, we have:

> *Why should we worship God enthusiastically?*
> *Because he is a Good Shepherd.*

The tension is inherent in the thesis. The psalm is calling us to do something that we can't do, we don't want to do, or we don't know how to do—unless of course we understand the reason for it, which the psalm will proceed to unpack for us. We will see in the next chapter how to develop this into a sermon that capitalizes on building up and maintaining anticipation in the audience. For now, let's look at one more example of retrieving the thesis from a text, this time from the Gospels.

MATTHEW 5:1–12

This is the passage at the beginning of Jesus' Sermon on the Mount that contains the Beatitudes. The previous paragraph deals with Jesus' teaching and healing ministry among the crowds. The opening verse gives us a peek into the content of Jesus' teaching though it does not focus on the healing aspect of Jesus' ministry. So it seems like a clean enough break from the preceding material to see the pericope, or unit, starting here. Now you need to decide how much ground to cover in the Sermon on the Mount. It spans three chapters, so most likely you will want to treat it in parts. You will have to select your zoom level. When I preached this, I wanted to spend one sermon on 5:13–16 dealing with the salt and light metaphors. I felt it was important for my church to hear a message focused on our presence in the world and the kind of effect it should have. This unit is directly related to verses 1–12, as we will see in a moment, but it is just distinct enough that it can be handled separately without a straight repetition of the previous unit's thesis. The Beatitudes leave the preacher with much to unpack, and probably most Christians familiar with this passage see this as essentially a unit already. So I decided, for that particular sermon series, to preach Matthew 5:1–12 as a unit.

Let's briefly run through our thesis questions:

- ***What does this passage reveal to us about God?*** We know that Jesus comes on the scene teaching in such a way that the people were astonished at his authority (7:28–29). Through Jesus, we are getting the right perspective on all that God had revealed in the Law and the Prophets (5:17). Here we are learning what kind of life God expects of us; the kind of person the Lord blesses.

- ***What does this passage reveal to us about ourselves, and how we should respond to God?*** We may not readily see the value of spiritual poverty, mourning, or meekness. This requires a major recalibration of our hearts. Jesus is calling "blessed" what we might describe as cursed. The passage is equipping us by turning our value system on its head.

- ***How does this passage in particular drive these truths home to the reader?*** Jesus uses irony in his reversals of fortune. It is those who have nothing who will inherit everything. It is those who mourn who will experience comfort. It is not the conquerors and the fighters but the meek and the peacemakers who will inherit the earth and be called sons of God. The repetition of "blessed" is a distinct feature that delivers the burden of this passage to the reader. The thesis statement will certainly reflect this emphasis. It also bases today's blessedness on a future hope.

- ***If this passage did not exist, what profit would we be missing?*** Other portions of the Sermon on the Mount focus on rightly living the intent of the Law and the Prophets. But this passage particularly spotlights the counterintuitiveness of kingdom values. Here we have a unique introduction to not just kingdom ethics in general but their irony, as well as the juxtaposition of our present experience with our future reality.

- ***What problem or question is the passage solving or answering? What issue is it addressing?* (You are looking for the *subject*.)** "Blessedness" in this context is referring to a joyous state of favor in God's eyes.[49] I would explain this in the sermon and use "joy" to make an easier connection with today's audience. "Rejoice and be glad" repeats the sentiment and therefore gives explicit precedent for using "joy" in a synonymous way with "blessedness." So our subject has something to do with experiencing this joy of God's divine favor.

Furthermore, I see that while the Beatitudes can be applied broadly, they are dealing specifically with the difficulty of living under persecution for following Christ, particularly in his mission. I see this because in the preceding verses Jesus' ministry is defined as preaching repentance and the kingdom of heaven (4:17) and he calls disciples to join him in this task (v. 19). He then continues to proclaim the gospel throughout Galilee (v. 23). It seems that to be a disciple is to join Jesus in this gospel-proclaiming endeavor. Mark does the same thing in the opening chapter of his gospel. But disciples, as gospel-proclaimers through word and action, will be persecuted for it. The final beatitude explicitly refers to this reality (5:10). The previous beatitudes are not

---

49. The term *makarios* appears fifty times in the New Testament and is used almost exclusively for "religious joy" (W. D. Davies and D. C. Allison, *The Gospel According to Saint Matthew*, vol. 1, International Critical Commentary [New York: T&T Clark, 1988]), 434. This interpretation is also made on the basis of Hebrew parallels in the Old Testament where the idea behind "blessed" is that all will go well for those who live for God (Grant R. Osborne, *Matthew*, Zondervan Exegetical Commentary on the New Testament, [Grand Rapids: Zondervan, 2010]), 165.

separate realities but rather parallel each other. They speak to the difficulty of living the Christian life. It is difficult precisely because of worldly opposition. Rather than warring against it in zealous anger, we must respond in meekness, mercy, and peacemaking. Yes, sometimes we will experience loss and we will mourn. But if we remain pure in heart and poor in spirit, we will inherit the kingdom. Jesus ends the list with persecution and expounds it, making it clear this is the climax of the beatitudes (5:11–12). Verses 11–12 function as a sort of interpretation of the preceding verses. Persecution for following Christ is the crux of the passage. Of course, the unit that follows confirms the theme: We will experience the temptation to hide in this world, but as salt cannot hide its effects and neither can light, we must have our effect on this world. The proclamation of the gospel (4:17–19) and the good works that prove it is a reality in our lives (5:16).

Thus, the subject for this passage can be stated as: *We can joyfully endure persecution.* Using the word "can" strikes that note of hope that we see throughout the unit. Living like this, though counterintuitive, is possible. It is possible to live under persecution *joyfully blessed*. Our next question asks how.

- ***What solution or answer does the passage offer with regard to the primary issue it is addressing?* (You are looking for the *complement*.)** If the primary issue being addressed is living joyfully under persecution, what is Jesus saying about the issue? How does Jesus resolve the problem? The tension is that we don't know how to experience joy under such circumstances. We don't understand how one can feel blessed or joyous when experiencing the misery of the world's opposition. Jesus' answer is

> that there is an inheritance awaiting us. We are blessed now not because of any current experience but because of a future one. We experience joy now and in eternity because our inheritance is secured by Christ. This inheritance cannot be robbed or taken from us. So the complement can be stated this way: *because of what is secured for later* or, to be more specific, *because our inheritance is secured for later*. This thesis statement essentially matches each Beatitude:
>
> *Blessed are those who live like this,*
> *because they will experience that.*
>
> Our thesis statement reflects that pattern:
>
> *We can joyfully endure persecution,*
> *because our inheritance is secured for later.*
>
> I am using the word "later" to emphasize the "shall" of each beatitude. That while we must mourn now, we *shall* inherit the earth, we *shall* have the kingdom, we *shall* see God.

Unlike the Judges example, in both of the above, I did not really need to universalize the sermon thesis. For Psalm 100, we all praise God and we all do it because he is good. If there was something specific to temple worship that does not translate to our experience, for instance, we would have had to state the thesis more universally. Similarly, the thesis statement for Matthew 5:1–12 translates directly to the Christian experience in every place and time, though persecution levels vary. Still, the point of anticipation and arrival works for today's audiences as it did for yesterday's. For Psalm 100, we need to find joy in worship when we often feel dry and perfunctory. We need a grander vision of the Lord's goodness. For Matthew 5:1–12, we find it difficult to live as meek, peacemaking Christians in a world of opposition. We want to feel secure (or blessed) by making ourselves as comfortable here as we can, even if we have to fight for it. But we must not. The solution to living in meekness is the promise of the kingdom inheritance. The sermon will take the listener on a journey from discovering the need to the solution that the text offers. When this thread of anticipation is maintained, attention will not be easily lost.

CONCLUSION

A sermon's thesis statement carries tension when it contains a clear subject and complement or, if you will, a problem and solution. There is a need that is being addressed. There is a belief that is being reinforced or a misunderstanding that is being corrected. Some behavior that is being encouraged or rebuked. If the main idea of the sermon captures the agenda of the text, then the main idea will always carry tension in some form. Before the preacher begins outlining his sermon, the question must be asked: "What problem is being addressed here?" The preacher must have an unambiguous answer to that question. It should be clear what the burden of the sermon is or what it is trying to accomplish. And that burden should match the burden of the text. The problem states why the listener must go on this journey with the preacher, and the solution is the destination to which they are headed. This is tension.[50]

---

50. This would be a good time to take a look at Exercise 1 Practice: Determining Thesis Statements on page 161. Take your time with each one and don't fret if yours looks a little different than mine. But try to identify the components: the subject and the complement.

Once you have a clear, succinct thesis statement, you still need to decide which way you will structure the sermon. Without a clear structure that is strategically chosen and designed for maintaining the sermon's point of tension, it will be difficult to keep an audience listening no matter how clear or compelling the thesis statement. We must become proficient at shaping our sermons effectively.

CHAPTER 3

Determine the Structure

Great expository content without a good delivery plan will amount to a poor sermon. At a joint church service where several congregations were represented, I was responsible for presiding over the Lord's Supper. This was, unfortunately, placed in the middle of the preacher's sermon. The plan was that he would stop somewhere in the middle of his message, I would lead the gathering in communion, and then he would finish the last half of his sermon. I needed to know the midpoint of the sermon so I would know when to step in. As we were coordinating with the sound team beforehand I asked him, "Halfway through your sermon, what signal can you give me that lets me know I should be ready to come up?" He wasn't sure. So I thought I'd make it easy, and I told him to just tell me the last point he would be making before I should come up. He didn't know. I said, "I see you are using slides tonight—which slide would you say is around the middle of your sermon? I'll see the slide and know I'm about to be up." He couldn't tell me. I don't remember how long it took me to realize it, but as he flipped through his stack of notes and slide printouts, it became obvious he had no clue where the middle of his sermon was. There was no middle because there was no plan, no structure. This man was not unlearned and he had good content. But it was a very confusing sermon. When he preached, we were all lost because *he* was lost.

I felt bad for him because I've been there many times. I spend time excavating Scripture for its invaluable gold, but when I fail to invest time into figuring out how I am going to deliver this treasure to my listeners they disengage quickly. They are lost because I'm lost.

Good leaders know where they are going. But it's not enough to know where they are going—they need to know how they are getting there. They need a route as well as a destination. This is true whether backpackers are being led on a thru-hike along a mountain trail or an organization is being led through a corporate merger. In a sermon, the audience has some understanding of a subject and the preacher seeks to lead them to a new, renewed, or different understanding of that subject. How will the preacher get them there? Every preacher needs a plan. Without one, the audience will be lost somewhere along the way. If preachers are not sure *how* they are going where they are going, it will be very difficult for any audience to stay with them.

This is especially critical when developing a sermon that centers on one thesis. And it is even more critical for the preacher seeking to sustain listener interest with tension. Many of us have been groomed to explain a verse, illustrate it, and apply it, then do it all again for the next verse—that's the map we've been given for every Scripture. It's an outline, but it's not really a map. There's not really a singular destination. It's here and it's there. What we're looking to do is create a path for tension in the sermon. To do this, we must articulate an overarching question.

THE OVERARCHING QUESTION

The structure (or outline) of the sermon is the route that the preacher uses to teach the primary idea while maintaining tension. Each successive stage of the sermon should take the tension that has been developed early on and move it toward resolution. The greater the clarity of the thesis and its inherent tension, the greater the clarity you will have on how to plot your route.

It is the very singularity of the one-sentence thesis statement that allows the preacher to create a clear, memorable outline. Consider William Zinsser's thoughts concerning the task of writing:

> As for what point you want to make, every successful piece of nonfiction should leave the reader with one provocative thought that he or she didn't have before. Not two thoughts, or five—just one. So decide what single point you want to leave in the reader's mind. It will not only give you a better idea of what route you should follow and what destination you hope to reach; it will affect your decision about tone and attitude.[51]

Singularity of purpose gives the author a better idea of what route to take. It is no different for the preacher.

So at this point you are armed with a clear thesis, and you are in search of a good route to take in delivering it. But it needs to be a direct route; otherwise your audience will see you like the tedious conversation partner who has a point but is taking the long way to get there. You will find this direct route with the guidance of an *overarching question*.

---

51. William Zinsser, *On Writing Well: The Classic Guide to Writing Nonfiction*, 6th ed. (New York: HarperCollins, 2001), 53.

The overarching question is the written expression of the tension in the sermon. The preacher will want to write down and articulate exactly what the tension is in his message. What burning question is the scriptural author striving to answer? What difficult problem will this text resolve for the reader? What theological quandary does this passage solve? This is the question burning inside your listener after your introduction. This is the question the text is going to answer. This question is the whole point of the sermon and why they must listen.

The overarching question is not the same as the sermon's thesis; it takes the thesis statement's inherent tension and puts it into the form of a question. What is being promised in the introduction? What are we telling them the text is going to deliver for them? Articulating this question will allow the preacher to understand why the listener should be enthusiastically tuning in for the sermon. We do not devise a random overarching question that we think might sound good. Rather, we discern the overarching question in our thesis statement.

The reason it is an *overarching* question is because it does not get answered immediately. It takes a significant chunk of the sermon, if not the entire sermon, to answer it. This is different from simply asking a question in your introduction and promising the answer by the end. In that scenario, you are essentially offering the audience a trade: "If you want the answer to this question, please lend me your attention for the duration of the sermon and then in the end I will give it to you." In this case, the question may or may not be relevant to the big idea of the sermon. We've gone back to a gimmicky way of holding attention. Instead, the overarching question not only draws the audience into the sermon but the answer is unfolded in the sermon bit by bit until the resolution is full and complete. Every piece of the sermon is relevant to it.

There are essentially two ways to find the overarching question from your thesis. The first way is to turn your subject into a question (as we have seen in the previous chapter). The complement will be your answer, and the subject is the question that will drive that sermon. The route you choose will be one that allows the text to, little by little, collect the evidence needed to deliver the verdict: your complement. If you are preaching on Mark 2:1–12 concerning Jesus' healing of the paralytic, your thesis might be: *We can trust Christ's authority to forgive sins because he is God.* Your subject can be stated as a question: *How can I trust Christ to truly forgive my sins?* You would walk your audience through the verses explaining how this question is burning in the text. It will take you time to unpack the answer as you work through the nuances of the passage. Jesus doesn't say *directly* that he is God, but he declares it still. As you prove this, you will eventually bring your audience to the same conclusion you came to in your study—that Jesus' forgiveness is totally trustworthy because he has total authority to grant it.

The other way to find your overarching question is to see what question is prompted by your thesis statement. Rather than turning your subject into a question, you will see the entire thesis (subject and complement) as prompting a deeply felt question. Let's imagine you are preaching Psalm 23 and your thesis is: *When the Lord is your Shepherd, you will be completely satisfied.* You might anticipate that there could be an objection to this. Your listener might be thinking, "I've been following Christ for thirty-five years, but my life is falling apart and I am feeling far from satisfied." They see the subject and complement but they don't believe it or understand it adequately. You can even vocalize this concern—you probably should. Make the point of tension clear. You might write down the overarching question as: *If the Lord's shepherding eliminates all want, why do I feel so wanting?* Then the sermon will walk the audience through Psalm 23 and, piece by piece, demonstrate to them that truly the Lord is an all-satisfying shepherd, even in the darkest valleys.

The overarching question, derived from your thesis statement, will keep your direction sharp. Articulating it will help you move along in the sermon by knowing how you are bringing your listeners along with you. It will help keep you from meandering. You won't be lost and neither will your audience.

STRUCTURING YOUR SERMON FOR TENSION

Once you have both your thesis and your overarching question clearly articulated, you will need to decide how you are going to structure the sermon to unfold it. Plotting the course your sermon will take gives it the shape or structure it needs. There are four basic patterns the preacher can follow to do this. These are not the only patterns, but they will provide some foundational avenues to get to your destination. Once these four are mastered, all sorts of hybrids and exceptions can be introduced.

In *Biblical Preaching,* Haddon Robinson explains the differences and advantages of these four basic sermonic structures.[52] I tried to use them for many years but was never really successful until I understood the role of tension, especially as articulated in an overarching question. Choosing your sermon structure is crucial because it will represent how tension in the sermon is managed—how the overarching question will function. Because tension has to do with movement—movement from a question toward an answer—understanding the sermon's structure is important. Dennis Cahill, author of *The Shape of Preaching*, elaborates:

52. Robinson, *Biblical Preaching*, 117.

> Related to movement is the issue of tension. Tension is the unresolvedness of the sermon. Tension is what keeps the listeners on the edge of their seats; it keeps them listening. This tension is what Eugene Lowry calls ambiguity. Questions are asked but not answered. Problems are explored but not solved. Issues are raised but not resolved. Some sermons state the central idea early in the sermon and then ask questions about that idea, questions that simply must be answered. Other sermons develop tension by not revealing the full central idea until the end of the sermon.[53]

The movement from problem to solution will not work the same way in every sermon. The way tension will work will differ depending on the structure chosen. But understanding tension is key to understanding why one will work better than another. Without the overarching question, it will be difficult to know which structure to use and how to use it.

Here are the four:

- *The INDUCTIVE structure.* The thesis statement is fully revealed at the *end.*
- *The DEDUCTIVE structure.* The thesis statement is fully revealed at the *beginning.*
- *The INDUCTIVE-DEDUCTIVE structure.* The thesis statement is fully revealed in the *middle.*
- *The SUBJECT-COMPLETED structure.* The subject of the thesis is revealed at the *beginning* and is completed with two or more complements throughout,

53. Dennis M. Cahill, *The Shape of Preaching: Theory and Practice in Sermon Design* (Grand Rapids: Baker, 2007), 117.

or the entire thesis is revealed at the beginning and the original complement is expanded in two or more complements throughout.

We will look at these in turn and see how the overarching question carries tension forward in each of them. The key difference between them is where the thesis statement is fully revealed: at the end, at the beginning, or in the middle.

THE INDUCTIVE STRUCTURE

The *inductive structure* lends itself most naturally to preaching with tension precisely because it begins with a question and works toward the answer in the end. The inductive approach does not begin with the full thesis. With the inductive pattern the listener does not get the full big idea until the end of the sermon. The preacher begins with a question and during the course of the sermon gradually moves the listener toward the answer. The primary advantage of the inductive sermon is that it most naturally sets up tension for the listeners. As Donald Sunukjian explains, "It more easily sustains the tension or suspense to the end of the message. The listener has to keep listening since the answer, or take-home truth, is still ahead."[54] For most preachers, generating and sustaining tension will be easiest in the inductive structure.

SETTING UP THE OVERARCHING QUESTION WITH THE INDUCTIVE STRUCTURE

To get the overarching question in an inductive sermon, pose the subject of your thesis in question form. The subject is the

---

54. Donald R. Sunukjian, *Invitation to Biblical Preaching: Proclaiming Truth with Clarity and Relevance* (Grand Rapids: Kregel, 2007), 154.

question, and the complement is the answer. If you have already articulated your thesis statement in this way, then this step has already been done. In the inductive sermon, the complement will be gradually revealed throughout the exposition and fully revealed in the end.

For example, take a simple thesis statement for an oral presentation: *Fishing is challenging because it requires patience*. The subject can be stated in question form: *Why is fishing challenging?* The answer is the complement: *Because it requires patience.* The speaker would set up the subject as the overarching question that will carry the entire speech. The beginning of the speech would perhaps give some examples of frustrating experiences with fishing. Then the question would be posed to the audience: *Why is fishing so challenging?* The speaker then promises, explicitly or implicitly, that the rest of the speech will answer that question. By the end they will have the answer: *Because it requires patience.*

Or let's say we take Ecclesiastes 3:1–15 as a preaching unit and our thesis statement looks something like this: *Even though life seems random and purposeless, we can enjoy it because God is in charge of it*. It can be broken down like this:

Subject: *How can we enjoy life when it seems so random and purposeless?*

Complement: *Because God is in charge of it.*

An inductive sermon would have the subject as the overarching question right at the outset, but the answer would be withheld. The preacher would promise the listeners that the text will provide the answer as it is investigated. In this sermon the preacher would spend time driving home the subject, which will continually press the question. The details of the text will underscore the perspective that life is random, cyclical, and seemingly without purpose. The listeners would then tune in more attentively as their interest has been piqued by the introduction and enhanced by the expounding of the subject in the text. The answer will then be provided toward the end of the sermon, once all the clues have been collected and explained. Throughout the inductive sermon we are moving toward the answer bit by bit, but the full answer is not delivered explicitly until the end.

In figure 3.1, you will see an overview of what the basic outline might look like for an inductive sermon on Ecclesiastes 3:1–15.[55] Notice that the main movements of the sermon serve to progressively answer the overarching question (OQ). The first stop along the way is to affirm the problem; the second is to challenge our understanding of the problem by providing the author's different perspective. Then, third, we see the author's desire for the reader—but we still don't know how to live like that. The fourth and final stop is the full reveal. We get the complement that answers the subject. Here the audience gets the entire thesis statement (TS) for the first time.

The inductive structure reveals a piece at a time, moving the listener toward the complement, the answer. In the above figure, the preacher establishes the subject and lets the audience feel the brunt of its brutality. Surprisingly, the author sees beauty in the seemingly random cycles even though he just wondered out loud what gain could possibly be had in anyone's toil given the random seasons that produce no progress. This piques our curiosity. We know there's a resolution in the author's mind, but we don't know how he got there yet. Then he reveals his

---

55. I have also included a more detailed outline of an inductive sermon on Ecclesiastes 7:1–2 in Appendix C on page 202.

Ecclesiastes 3:1–15

Inductive Structure

Introduction

Subject: *How can we enjoy life when it seems so random and purposeless?*

(This is the OQ.)

Body

I. Life can feel random and purposeless because of its cyclical nature (3:1–9, cf. 1:1–11)

II. The author sees beauty in the cycles even though God frustrates man's desire to know their purpose (3:10–11).

III. His conclusion is we should take joy in our toil even though we do not know the purpose of every season (3:12–13).

IV. **TS**: We can enjoy life even when it seems random and purposeless because God is in charge of it (3:14–15).

Conclusion

Figure 3.1

conclusion about the whole matter: we should take joy and pleasure in our seemingly vain toil. But he doesn't quite give the reason yet. Then finally, in the last couple of verses in this unit, he explains that it is God's sovereignty that provides comfort in the midst of our confusion over life and its cycles. They aren't random. They are purposed. And God knows what he is doing.

TROUBLESHOOTING THE INDUCTIVE STRUCTURE

One difficulty that preachers will encounter with the inductive structure is that the answer will often arise in the text sooner than the end of the passage. You thought the inductive pattern would work, but it really doesn't. The inductive pattern is meant to unfold or develop the complement in waves until it is clear by the end. But, when looking at the text, if you see that the answer appears sooner than the end of the passage, it may be that the inductive-deductive pattern is the better option.

The inductive pattern is also sometimes misunderstood. In an inductive sermon, each step along the way adds a piece to the puzzle. As I warned above when introducing the overarching question, it is not that the preacher begins with a question, promises the answer, and then embarks on an irrelevant journey just to come back around to the original question at the end. Rather, each part of the sermon works to bring the listener to a kind of gestalt—a sense of the whole. Each piece of the sermon works to provide the answer that the individual piece could not fully give on its own.

Some preachers feel the only way to preach with tension is to preach inductively. As a result, they tend to favor narrative portions of Scripture, or perhaps they begin every sermon with a question as their opening line and proceed from there. Indeed, it is true that parables, narratives, and apocalyptic passages lend themselves to the inductive route quite nicely. You can also use it when the thesis statement works really well as a question and answer (that is, the subject can be stated as a *provocative* question as opposed to a question we all feel we already know the answer to). But it isn't necessary to be exclusively committed to the inductive structure. Tension is possible in the other patterns as well, and some texts are better suited to them.

THE DEDUCTIVE STRUCTURE

The *deductive structure* begins with the entire thesis statement up front, somewhere in the sermon's introduction. The rest of the sermon proceeds to elaborate on it or argue it. Whereas the inductive pattern begins with a question (the subject) and moves toward the answer (the complement), the deductive sermon presents the full thesis at the front end (both subject and complement). Since in this kind of sermon the thesis is stated in the introduction and is repeated throughout the entire message, the advantage of the deductive sermon is clarity.[56]

Because the deductive structure does not lend itself as naturally to the development of tension, I will devote more space to it than to the inductive structure. With the deductive pattern, tension cannot work the way it works in the inductive approach. The problem and solution have been stated together at the front end. There is no waiting for the complement. Tension, however, can still be developed.

This is a typical approach for newspaper and magazine articles. Journalism professor Peter Jacobi encourages writers of news stories to use a deductive pattern (what he refers to as an inverted pyramid).[57] This means that the reader gets the main point right away. Philip Gerard explains that in the news stories using the deductive pattern, the lead sentence "answers the most important mystery right off the bat."[58] This is because news stories typically begin with a shocking or startling lead that reveals the "punch." Why would news stories give the entire "big idea"

---

56. Sunukjian, *Invitation to Biblical Preaching*, 149.

57. Peter P. Jacobi, *The Magazine Article: How to Think It, Plan It, Write It* (Cincinnati: Writer's Digest Books, 1991), 63.

58. Philip Gerard, *Creative Nonfiction: Researching and Crafting Stories of Real Life* (Cincinnati: Story Press, 1996), 166.

away right at the beginning? Don't they want the reader to read the rest of the article? Yes, but revealing the punch at the top is precisely what draws the reader in.

Readers know the primary idea but still read with interest. They continue to read because the idea has generated some question (or questions) in their minds that they are now eager to have answered. If the headline reads, "Eight Firefighters Killed in Unstoppable Brush Fire," the reader has the main idea. The subject is "eight firefighters have been killed." The complement is "by a brush fire that cannot be stopped." The answer is given immediately, yet the reader feels compelled to keep reading because another question has been prompted. It might be, "What manner of brush fire is this that it cannot be put out?" Or it might be, "Am I in danger if this fire is not put out soon?" The deductive statement, though it is the full idea, causes the reader to demand more. In order for this to work, the beginning has to be shocking, disruptive, startling, or curious. Thus a headline reading, "Apples Are Healthy to Eat" would generate little interest—it is not news. "Apples Discovered to Cure Cancer"—that is front-page worthy.

When Dennis Cahill discusses the deductive form, he admits that at first glance it seems to resolve all of the tension up front. But pressing questions can be asked.[59] He refers to Haddon Robinson, who teaches that deductive patterns can maintain the necessary tension by asking questions that *explain*, *prove*, or *apply* the big idea stated up front.[60] But this is difficult to do without a clear overarching question.

---

59. Dennis M. Cahill, *The Shape of Preaching: Theory and Practice in Sermon Design* (Grand Rapids: Baker, 2007), 117.

60. Robinson, *Biblical Preaching*, 118–23.

SETTING UP THE OVERARCHING QUESTION WITH THE DEDUCTIVE STRUCTURE

To set up the overarching question using a deductive structure, begin with a thesis statement that demands explanation or proof.[61] The subject and complement are both revealed, but in a way that demands more. The thesis is presented in a way that raises a question in the mind of the listener: "How so?" (explanation) or "Can you prove that?" (proof).[62]

Let's take James 1:1–18 as our sample passage here with the thesis stated this way: *We should rejoice in suffering* (subject) *because it perfects us* (complement). The passage hints at a deductive pattern because both the subject and the complement are revealed in the second sentence of the passage. Not only is the complement revealed very early; the subject and complement are provocative. The thesis easily prompts a question in the mind of the average listener. Whereas in the inductive structure you turn your subject into a question and that becomes your overarching question, in the deductive structure you get your overarching question by putting into words the confusion, hesitation, or objection that the listener most likely has in response to the thesis.

It would look like this:

Thesis: *We should rejoice in suffering because it perfects us.*
Overarching Question: *How so?* (for example)

61. Robinson includes application as a way to develop big ideas deductively, but for the purposes of this chapter we will focus on explanation and proof.

62. Perhaps no single source explains the difference between the inductive and deductive patterns more clearly than Donald Sunukjian's *Invitation to Biblical Preaching*, 142–60.

The overarching question in this case can take various forms in the minds of the listeners: "How is that possible?" "I don't see how that's true—can you prove that?" "Where does the Bible say that?" "I know I'm supposed to believe that, but how does that work? How does that make sense?" "Why would God demand that of me?" The preacher might even vocalize some of these questions before moving into the body of the sermon, but the preacher focuses on one overarching question that represents them all. The thesis statement, fully stated, heightens tension. The answer is provided in the complement, but that very answer sparks another question. It will be a question that demands proof or explanation, and it will carry tension the rest of the way.[63]

In figure 3.2, you can see that the introduction brings the audience to the full thesis statement. The impact of the thesis is felt as the preacher presses the tension. This prompts the audience's thinking: "How?" The body of the sermon consists of the preacher using the text to answer that question. The expositor looks for how *James* answers the overarching question and unpacks it for the listeners in the way that he does.

This means the introduction is key. In order for the deductive structure to work, the preacher will need to introduce the thesis statement in a way that heightens the demand for either proof or explanation. Using our James 1:1–18 example, an introduction that sets up the demand for *explanation* might look something like this:

> Suffering affects all of us. None of us is immune. We might suffer at different levels, but trials are inevitable.

---

63. For more on how the deductive pattern works to generate questions, see especially Donald Sunukjian, *Invitation to Biblical Preaching*, 156–59. Also, Dennis Cahill, *The Shape of Preaching*, 115–27.

James 1:1–18
Deductive Structure

Introduction	TS: *We should rejoice in suffering because it perfects us.* (OQ: How is this so?)
Body	I. It is a perfection born from steadfastness—thus trials are necessary (1:2–4). II. We may find it impossible to count trials as joy—thus we must ask for wisdom (1:5–8). III. We will experience lows because it is the lowly who are exaclted in trials (1:9–15). IV. God is perfecting us as first fruits of his creation (1:16–18).
Conclusion	

Figure 3.2

Most of us would think life would be perfect if some monumental difficulty in our life would just go away. If that disease would just be healed; if that promotion would just come through; if that spouse would only change. Life would be perfect. But that's not what Scripture says. In fact, it says the opposite. The Bible tells us we should rejoice in suffering because without it, life would be less than perfect. We would be less perfect than we already

> are. But *with* suffering, we are made perfect. God allows a life-threatening disease? I'm brought closer to perfection. Job loss? More perfection. Tough marriage? Closer to perfection still. We shouldn't just accept suffering; we should count it as a joyous occasion! *We should rejoice in suffering because it perfects us.*

Such an introduction expresses the full thesis statement more than once. Yet tension is generated in that the listeners are beginning an internal monologue where they are asking for an explanation. "How do these devastating trials make me perfect?" An introduction like this sets the thesis up in a way that demands explanation. The need for the explanation is the source of tension. The overarching question is, "How is that so?"

Another way to set up a deductive sermon on James 1:1–18 is to heighten the demand for *proof*. To do this the preacher will cast the thesis in a way that capitalizes on the doubt of the hearers. The introduction might look something like this:

> The Bible tells us to rejoice in pain. To count suffering as an occasion for joy. But that sounds incredible, doesn't it? You who have been believers for a while, you've seen this right? Right there in James 1:2 we read, "Count it all joy, my brothers, when you meet trials of various kinds." Notice he doesn't say, "Accept all your trials" or "Put up with all your trials"—no, he says, "Count them all as joy." Do you believe that? We all know we're supposed to believe that because it's in the Bible. But search deeply. Honestly. When I am diagnosed with a life-threatening disease—count it as joy? When I am escorted out of my building with all my belongings in a box because I have been let go—yay! Really? When my marriage is

> so strained I don't know how we're going to make it—rejoice? Is this verse for real? Does God really expect me to rejoice in my devastating trials? If we are to take Scripture seriously we have to grapple with this verse. *We should rejoice in suffering because it perfects us.*

In this example, the preacher comes right out and says what everyone is probably thinking in response to the thesis—the preacher asks the question for them: "Does God really expect me to rejoice in my devastating trials?"

To be clear, the demand for proof does not require that the preacher vocalize the overarching question—it is merely an option. The preacher can choose to vocalize the overarching question in the first introduction example as well. In either case, the preacher is generating an overarching question outside of the thesis statement itself. Whether or not you ask the overarching question explicitly in your delivery, you should write it down during your sermon preparation. You need to have a clear and precise understanding of what you are answering in the sermon even if the question takes various forms in the minds of the listeners.

Some preachers who have favored the inductive structure because it more naturally keeps people's interest may feel averse to the deductive pattern. But the deductive structure is an effective option especially when the thesis statement is one that easily generates tension by itself. When the thesis statement is in some way surprising or intriguing, the deductive format can carry tension quite well.

TROUBLESHOOTING THE DEDUCTIVE STRUCTURE

Difficulties arise with the deductive pattern when the preacher chooses this structure unaware that it really will not work for the given sermon. The preacher did not think carefully enough about the implications concerning deductive preaching. To avoid this, we must recognize the signs that "greenlight" the deductive structure and only use it when we're given the "go."

As discussed earlier, the first sign that you should probably preach deductively is when the subject and complement are both given away early in the text. If your audience is following along with you in the passage, they are going to see it. In this case, go deductive. Just make sure you are setting up the thesis statement in a way that startles the audience or provokes curiosity—which leads to the next point.

One glaring "red light" that should stop you in your tracks if you're considering the deductive pattern is if your thesis statement will fall on the typical listener's ear as a tired platitude. If the thesis sounds trite, the deductive pattern is not going to work very well. Theses like, "*We should pray in order to grow spiritually,*" or "*Read your Bible every day because that is how we know God*" are not going to generate much tension when stated up front in the sermon. These kinds of statements are profound and may very well be evident in a given passage, but they are not *disruptive*. They are timeworn and predictable and lack any sense of "punch." There's no tension there.

When the Scripture passage works deductively but the thesis statement you've come up with sounds hackneyed or not very relevant, you might feel stuck. Let's say you have a thesis that looks something like: "*We should not worship idols because God is a jealous God.*" If the text is pointing you to a deductive sermon pattern, then you might want to rethink the wording of the thesis or at least how you're going to set it up. For example, if you are preaching in well-to-do suburban America, most folks in your church probably would not list idolatry in the top ten sins they battle. They don't have wooden carvings that they bow down to or other gods that they pray to. "Don't worship idols" is not news for them, so there is no tension. They don't want explanation or proof because they already agree.

What you need to do is spend some time setting up the thesis in the introduction. Tell them that while they think they are on board with this command they really are not. You don't explain exactly how yet. You just put forward your proposition that this is a command they are breaking. You tell them you know they don't have carvings that they bow down to. But you know this is still in their top ten list, or top three or, in actual fact, at number one. You include yourself—we are all idolaters. Then perhaps you reword the thesis a little, at least for the introduction: "*Each of us participates in idolatry that invokes God's jealousy*." As you unpack the Scripture passage, you apply it in a way that allows them to see this is not just about the ancient Israelites.

Here you are *proving* your thesis. You prove to them that they need to hear this sermon, you prove to them that they are in the same boat as the original audience of the passage, and you prove to them that God's jealousy is the reason we must change. "Don't worship idols" isn't a news flash, but "You are an idolater and God wants you to change" might be.

Oftentimes you will encounter a passage that will not really allow for a pure inductive or deductive outline and you will need to combine them. In that case, you're going to need the inductive-deductive structure.

THE INDUCTIVE-DEDUCTIVE STRUCTURE

The *inductive-deductive structure* is, as its name indicates, a hybrid of the inductive and deductive structures. It begins as an inductive sermon, but once the thesis statement is fully revealed there is more proving or explaining to do. The thesis does not have to appear in the exact middle of the sermon's body, but it is not revealed in the introduction (as you would in a deductive sermon), and it is not revealed at the very end (as you would in an inductive sermon). Where exactly the full thesis is revealed within the body of the sermon will be normally be determined by the text of Scripture. When the subject's complement becomes evident in the exposition of the text, the preacher will clearly express the full thesis at that point in the sermon. Another factor will be how much explanation or proof the thesis will demand. This might make the deductive portion shorter or longer, depending on what is needed.

SETTING UP THE OVERARCHING QUESTION WITH THE INDUCTIVE-DEDUCTIVE STRUCTURE

For the inductive-deductive structure, the overarching question will be produced in the same way as in the inductive structure. The preacher will turn the subject into a question and lead with that. We looked at Matthew 5:1–12 in the previous chapter, but let's take the next unit for our example here.

For a sermon on Matthew 5:13–16, I wrote down the following thesis statement: *We can effectively reach unbelievers with the gospel when they witness our good works*. I begin by introducing the subject as a question just as I would in any inductive sermon: *How can we be effective in reaching unbelievers with the gospel?* Every inductive-deductive structure will begin this way. Somewhere in the body of the sermon, however, the question is definitively answered. Perhaps you see that it would be difficult to keep the question lingering for long, so rather than forcing a delay, you reveal it. In this case, the answer comes at the end of the passage: *It is when they witness our good works.* This is the answer (the complement). Yet even though the answer is revealed, the sermon is not over. I need to continue because even though the thesis statement is complete, it demands something further (like explanation or proof).

Once I reveal that effectiveness in reaching the lost with the gospel coincides with their witnessing good works in us, the listeners might wonder how that is so or if that really is so. *That means there is a new overarching question.* At this point you should pause and underscore the full thesis statement and then repeatedly emphasize the new source of tension (that of explanation or proof). After raising the new overarching question ("How so?" or "Can you prove that to me?"), you then go further into the text to explain or prove the complement that has been revealed. Many preachers will find that this structure becomes quite commonplace for them since it allows the big idea to be revealed anywhere in the body of the sermon.

In this case, I identified the new overarching question as one pertaining to explanation. It seems to me that we misunderstand the role of good works in reaching the unsaved. I see in the adjacent units the explanation we need. Jesus calls us to more than the staple good works of the external religionist. He is pointing to a thoroughgoing interiority of righteousness (5:21–22a, 27–28, 31–32). Not only that, but this internal goodness is proven most demonstrably under the weight of persecution—that's when the Beatitudes really shine (vv. 10–12). Thus, I begin the sermon with a question, answer it from the text, recognize that this answer prompts a new question, and then proceed to explain it from the surrounding text.

The outline would look like this:

Matthew 5:13–16

Inductive-Deductive Structure

Introduction

Subject: *How can we be effective in reaching unbelievers with the gospel?*

(This is the OQ.)

Body

I. We cannot separate gospel witness from discipleship (5:13–15).

TS: *We can effectively reach unbelievers with the gospel when they witness our good works.*

How is this so? (This the follow-up OQ.)

II. Jesus' idea of good works may be different from ours (5:16).

A. Good works reveal an internal righteousness (5:21–22a, 27–28, 31–32).

B. This internal righteousness is most obviously revealed in the shadow of persecution (5:10–12).

Conclusion

Figure 3.3

At this point you might be wondering how a sermon can have two overarching questions. If it is *overarching*, shouldn't it cover the entire sermon? In the other structures it does, but

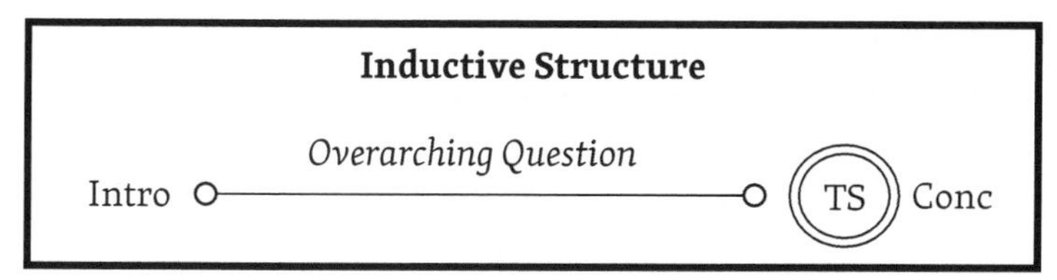

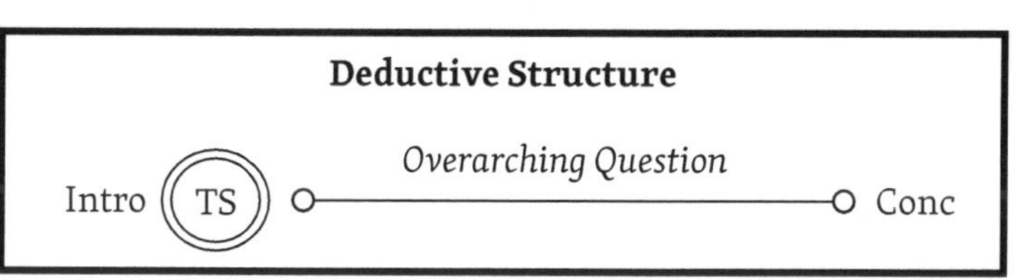

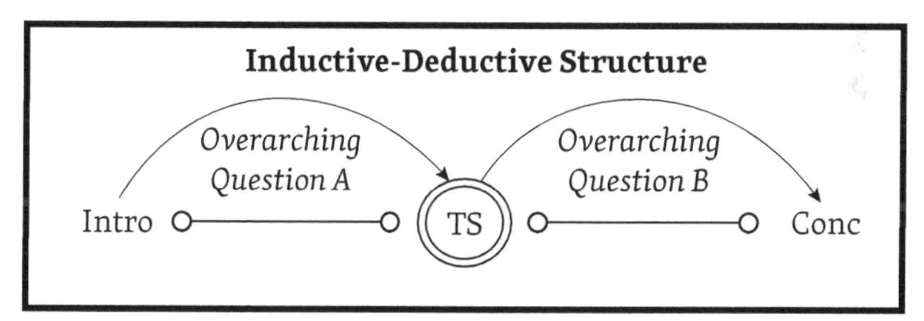

Figure 3.4

in this structure, you will have two—but they are "overarching" nonetheless, since they drive the tension in a major section of the sermon. In an inductive-deductive structure, the first overarching question carries tension for the inductive portion. The second overarching question carries tension for the deductive portion.

TROUBLESHOOTING THE INDUCTIVE-DEDUCTIVE STRUCTURE

This pattern can easily become the fallback for preachers because it is versatile. The full thesis statement can be revealed closer to the beginning, closer to the end, or in the exact middle of the sermon. Besides, most Scripture passages reveal the whole thesis before the very end if not right away. Yet there are times when the sermon would work better in a straight inductive or straight deductive structure, as explained above. Look to use the inductive-deductive pattern when the complement is revealed before the end *and* there is still something left to explain or prove from the text. It can even be text that has been covered, but now you go back and address the new overarching question by unpacking something the audience may have missed in the first pass through the verses.

Normally you will be able to use one of the three sermon patterns we have covered thus far. There will be times, however, when the text provides more than one complement to the subject, in which case you will want to use the subject-completed structure. This is the fourth and final sermon pattern that we will cover here.

THE SUBJECT-COMPLETED STRUCTURE

The subject-completed structure is one in which the subject is accompanied by multiple complements rather than only one. You decide to use this structure when you see that the text offers up more than one complement to the subject, so you design the sermon to reveal one complement at a time. Before discussing how to sustain tension with a subject-completed structure, it is important to note two dangers with this pattern: one exegetical and one homiletical. The exegetical danger is the temptation to rework every text of Scripture into a list of points when not every text works this way. The homiletical danger is that the preacher is robbed of the ability to use a tension strategy that comes more naturally in the inductive or deductive routes. There are times, however, when the text calls for a subject-completed form, and this does not mean tension must disappear from the sermon.

The subject-completed structure will, however, prove the most difficult for sustaining tension throughout the sermon. This is because once the thesis statement is completed with the first complement, the listener has to be won over again to hang in for the second—and then again for the third, or however many complements there are in the particular passage. In other words, the first complement will provide tension release. The listener experiences the satisfaction or the resolution that the complement provides. Then tension will need to be revived in order to best hold listeners' attention for the next complement. This can be difficult, but it is not impossible. It is also, at times, necessary. The advantage of this structure is that it helps the preacher honor the text when it is clear there are more complements than just one in the biblical author's mind.

SETTING UP THE OVERARCHING QUESTION WITH THE SUBJECT-COMPLETED STRUCTURE

A subject-completed structure can look like a variation of either an inductive or a deductive structure. It looks similar to an inductive structure when you simply make the subject your question and then introduce each complement as an answer to that question. At other times, you might find it effective to handle the subject-completed structure deductively. Much as you would for a deductive sermon, you will begin your subject-completed message with the entire thesis statement.

Let's take Galatians 6:1–5 as our text here:

> Brothers, if anyone is caught in any transgression, you who are spiritual should restore him in a spirit of gentleness. Keep watch on yourself, lest you too be tempted. Bear one another's burdens, and so fulfill the law of Christ. For if anyone thinks he is something, when he

> is nothing, he deceives himself. But let each one test his own work, and then his reason to boast will be in himself alone and not in his neighbor. For each will have to bear his own load.

The thesis can be stated like this: *When fellow Christians fall, we should restore them.* The sermon works deductively because it begins with the whole thesis statement. The subject is: *What should we do when fellow Christians fall?* The answer is provided before the end of the sermon's introduction: *We should restore them.* But then the preacher will demonstrate that this thesis prompts the overarching question, "How so?" The preacher can massage that question a bit by touching on the extremes many churches go to in treating "caught" Christians too harshly. The preacher is inviting the audience to feel the weight of the overarching question—how should we go about this restoration business in our churches? They have both the subject and the complement but now they need to hear an explanation as to how it is done. The complement in the thesis statement is incomplete. The answers are supplied by the text (and, indeed, these answers are how the preacher knows what overarching question to press in the introduction). We can see two *fuller* complements in this unit:

Complement #1: We should restore them gently (6:1a).
Complement #2: We should restore them carefully (6:1b–5).[64]

While this is an effective way to handle multiple complements, tension can easily dissipate when you have to introduce

64. One might see a third complement: *We should restore them humbly (6:3–5).* Yet it seems that Paul is saying that spiritual humility is *how* we are careful. Since I see the piece on humility in these verses as an elaboration of the warning to "keep watch" on ourselves in verse 1, I am folding verses 3–5 into the second complement.

the next one. Since listeners are getting an answer in the first complement, they may feel satisfied. In our current example, after the first complement they may be thinking, "See, I knew it—we need to be *gentle* with fallen brothers and sisters. We should just come alongside them and be kind. I am spiritually mature enough to be around them even in their weakness. All we need is love." They might be less eager to hear your second complement than they were to hear your first because they feel like they got the answer. You will need to show them why they are not yet finished listening to the text.

The way to sustain tension with a subject-completed structure is to supplement the overarching question with *incremental questions*. Wherever the sermon is moving from one complement to the next, turn those transitions into questions that support the overarching question. Really, transitions are more effective when stated as questions in *every* structure. But they are especially crucial when dealing with multiple complements. The preacher needs to revive the import of the overarching question by helping the listener understand that it is not enough to have the first complement. They need subsequent complements in order to have the full answer. Each complement is introduced by an incremental question except for the first one. The preacher can carry the tension from complement to complement by using incremental questions as transitions.

Peter Jacobi teaches his students that there is no better way to write an informative magazine article than to use progressive questions and answers.[65] For preachers, there is no better way to keep your listeners through a subject-completed message. Dealing with multiple complements is similar to the effective magazine article conveying various points of information. And,

---

65. Jacobi, *The Magazine Article*, 66–67.

as Jacobi points out, it will help engage the listener to revive tension with incremental questions along the way. An outline for a sermon on Galatians 6:1–5 using the subject-completed structure could look like this:

Galatians 6:1–5

Subject-Completed Structure

Introduction

TS: *When fellow Christians fall, we should restore them.*

(OQ: How should we restore them?)

Body

I. Complement #1: We should restore them gently (6:1a).

[Now prove this complement from the text.]

Incremental question: But how gentle should we be? (Other iterations: What does "gentle" mean when the person is adamant about their behavior? How deeply should I go into "their world" in order to reach them? How aggressively should I lower my standards in order to make them feel comfortable sharing with me?)

II. Complement #2: We should restore them carefully (6:1b–5)

[Now prove this complement from the text.]

Conclusion

Figure 3.5

Incremental questions can turn the subject-completed structure into a strength when it comes to tension. John Stott taught that all preaching should be dialogical in the sense that sermons should prompt questions in the listeners and then answer them, then do it again.[66] However, for these incremental questions to work well, they should not be answered too quickly. That is, though they are stated as deductive points (the preacher asks the incremental question, then answers it, then goes to the text),[67] the preacher must not answer the incremental question too hurriedly. Take a moment to revive the tension in the sermon; this will not happen if the answer is given too fast.

Winfred Neely explains that "our tendency is to rush past the question, or to fail to see that they are great Spirit given [*sic*] opportunities to arouse more interest, listener involvement, and learning."[68] We ruin tension by asking the question in one breath and then answering it in the next, like this: "We see that we're supposed to restore them gently, but just how gentle should we be? Well, not so soft that we are simply joining them in their ruin." The answer here comes too soon. A better way to allow the tension to build is to camp out on the question a little longer:

> We see that we're supposed to restore them gently, but just how gentle should we be? I mean, do I wait a long

---

66. John Stott, *Between Two Worlds: The Challenge of Preaching Today* (Grand Rapids: Eerdmans, 1982), 60–61.

67. Notice that if the preacher asks the incremental question, then goes to the text for explanation before giving the answer, this would set the complements up as inductive points. This is not recommended as it hampers clarity and makes it difficult for the listener to know what to look for when they go to the text. See Donald Sunukjian, *Invitation to Biblical Preaching* (288–94) for more on this.

68. Winfred Omar Neely, "Tension Management in Biblical Preaching: The Stuff of Listener Interest, Involvement, and Learning" (unpublished essay, Chicago, 2013), 8.

> time to discuss their sin? Do I ignore their sin? Would it be a good strategy to hang out with their crowd to show that I am not judgmental? We see the issue here. So many churches simply blast away at people so it's easy to see why we need the caution to be gentle. But gentleness can be its own extreme, can't it? We can be so gentle and soft that we end up losing sight of our mission—to restore them, not to join them! So not only must we be gentle; we must be very *careful*. Let's look at the rest of verse 1.

A transition like this will serve to help the reader see why this point is in the text. The preacher is not simply tacking on extra points to fill time. The scriptural author was not rambling. This next complement is necessary and the preacher is showing why.

Incremental questions are the effective transitions that allow tension to survive in a subject-completed structure.[69] Again, transitions in any sermon structure should be more than just review and preview ("We looked at _____; now we're going to see this_____"). Transitions like these orient the audience as to where they are in the flow of things. But they do little to keep them *wanting* to go there—to convince them they need this next point or move in the sermon. This kind of transition is never more needed than in a subject-completed structure.

To see the importance of effective transitions, imagine someone giving a simple instructional talk on how to make an ice cream sundae. One transition might look like this: "We covered ice cream, fruit, and syrups. Now we are going to finish it off with crushed peanuts." That is boring. It might be related to the subject (what makes a great-tasting sundae), but it is related in

---

69. See Donald Sunukjian's comments in *The Art & Craft of Biblical Preaching* (Grand Rapids: Zondervan, 2005) on how questions as transitions work to revive the attention of the listener (337–38).

an uninteresting way. It is just an item in a list. However, if we allow the transition to carry the weight of tension and not just information, the dynamic changes. Instead, at that same point the speaker might say:

> Now ice cream, fruit, and syrups are essential ingredients. But if we stop with those, we are missing something salty. We also need a contrast in texture, like something crunchy. And visually, we need to break up the monochromatic effect of the syrups. This is why we use crushed peanuts.

Transitions are necessary in every sermon pattern, but they are crucial in the subject-completed structure because they are the glue to the various pieces: the multiple complements.[70] They not only serve to review, but they also serve to *preview* the coming point.[71] However, they should explain not just *what* complement is coming next, but *why* that upcoming complement is necessary. The need is being raised again; tension is being renewed. The incremental questions serve to revive and sustain the tension in the overarching question (see figure 3.6).

---

70. Many preachers have tried to fix this sense of disconnection by using an organizational sentence, typically featuring a key word such as "three *aspects*" or "four *ingredients*"—the attempt is to bring the loosely related complements together in the minds of the listeners. But this is less necessary when there is a "hook" before each complement—a reason why the next one is needed. Perhaps an organizational sentence would function better at the end by means of review, but a map at the front end is not necessary when each step is a logical progression. An organizational sentence up front can also make tension more difficult to sustain much as when a movie trailer reveals every major plot movement in the film. See Greg Scharf, *Prepared to Preach: God's Work and Ours in Proclaiming His Word* (Christian Focus, 2010), 129–32 for no less than five dangers that come with using the organizational sentence.

71. Robinson, *Biblical Preaching*, 187.

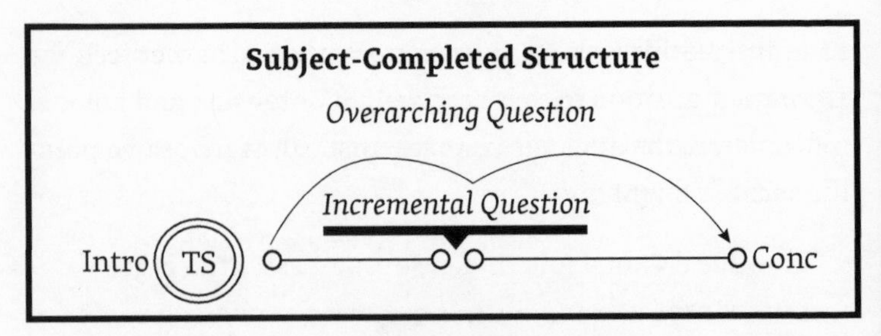

Figure 3.6

TROUBLESHOOTING THE SUBJECT-COMPLETED STRUCTURE

When using the subject-completed structure, we do not want it to seem like we have multiple thesis statements. This can happen when the complements seem arbitrarily connected. You should use incremental questions to show your listeners that there is a logical reason and, more importantly, a spiritual need for the next complement. You are not extending the sermon because you want to eat up time. You are extending it because there is more in the text, and there is more in the text because the Spirit inspired another complement to the subject. Show your listeners why in your incremental questions.

SELECTING A STRUCTURE FOR YOUR SERMON

Choosing a structure is essentially choosing where to reveal the thesis statement in full.[72] And that choice will alter the way tension is developed. All of these structures can carry tension, but they will do so differently because in each of them the thesis is revealed at a different time or in a different way. The inductive structure, for instance, functions like a classic "whodunit" mystery. Think of Sherlock Holmes beginning his investigation and

72. Sunukjian, *Invitation to Biblical Preaching*, 142.

little by little unraveling the mystery. By the end of the story, the identity of the murderer is revealed.

The deductive structure reverses that pattern, like a different kind of detective story. I grew up watching *Columbo*. Every episode begins with the answer—you see who the killer is, why they commit the crime, and how they do it. Why lean in and watch the rest of the episode? Because *Columbo* is not a "whodunit"; it's a "howcatchem."[73] This shows how tension is not only possible with the deductive format; it can at times be more effective.

The inductive-deductive structure functions more like an episode of *Law & Order*. The show always begins with the investigators trying to find the answer to the question: Who committed the crime? Partway through the show the criminal is found and arrested, but the episode is still not finished. The attorneys now have to *prove* that this person indeed committed the crime. In the inductive-deductive sermon the preacher gets the listener to the point where the complement (answer/solution) is revealed, but there is now something to explain or prove "in court" using the rest of the text or supplemental passages as the key witnesses.

Finally, the subject-completed structure tends to convey the thesis statement in a more informational way, much like a true crime documentary. Maybe the subject stays the same (one criminal or one kind of crime) but more than one complement is provided (the various crimes of the one criminal or the various criminals related to the one kind of crime). There is still a sense of mystery and intrigue, but it is more difficult to sustain than with the other structures. Nevertheless, when the text demands it, the preacher can still develop a subject-completed sermon in

---

73. Others have drawn this comparison. See Dennis M. Cahill, *The Shape of Preaching: Theory and Practice in Sermon Design* (Grand Rapids: Baker, 2007), 115–27; and Eugene L. Lowry, *The Homiletical Plot: The Sermon as Narrative Art Form* (Atlanta: John Knox Press, 1980), 79.

a way that maintains tension. There are boring documentaries and highly engaging documentaries. Subject-completed sermons can be done very well.

Understanding how the various structures function will help you make a strategic choice when preparing your sermon. The primary factor to consider when choosing a sermon structure is where in the text the thesis statement is fully revealed. As I explained above, it would be difficult to attempt an inductive pattern when the text reveals the complement in the first verse of the unit, for example. There are times for exceptions. You may find that the passage does not fit a clear pattern, or you might decide to move your listeners through the text out of order in order to communicate it more effectively. We will look at why these kinds of exceptions need to be made at the end of this chapter. But more often than not, the best pattern for the sermon will match the general pattern of the text. You will be able to identify the pattern that will fit best by recognizing the pattern the passage is favoring.

INDUCTIVE-FRIENDLY PASSAGES

How does a biblical text lend itself to an inductive sermon structure? Sometimes the text begins with an obvious question. Luke 18:18–30 is Jesus' response to the rich man's question about eternal life. Jesus responds to an overt question by the Sadducees concerning marriage in Luke 20:27–40. The book of Habakkuk starts out with the prophet's question about God's seemingly slow justice. But a passage may lend itself to an inductive structure even without an overt question. Psalm 50 begins with a description of God coming to rebuke his people. The question may be posed, "What is God upset about? Why is God coming as a fiery tempest? Why does he call on creation to witness the judgment of his people?" The rest of the psalm answers. *When you see that the passage immediately asks or prompts a question that the rest of the verses will answer, you should consider using an inductive pattern for your sermon.*

DEDUCTIVE-FRIENDLY PASSAGES

Passages that present both the subject and complement right away are passages that will best work with a deductive sermon pattern. Psalm 106 begins with a command to praise and give thanks to the Lord. There's your subject. Before leaving the first verse you also get the complement—*why* we should praise the Lord. *We should praise the Lord because his love is steadfast and endures forever.* The rest of the psalm proves this thesis. If you have 1 John 4:7–12 as your text, you will see that the first verse gives the primary point away: "Beloved, let us love one another, for love is from God, and whoever loves has been born of God and knows God." The succeeding verses explain that statement, but that first verse captures the primary truth: *We must love one another because that is what those who belong to God do.* Everything else in that passage helps us understand that opening line. A deductive sermon is effective when the thesis is presented in the text right away and then the rest of the passage elaborates on that thesis.

INDUCTIVE-DEDUCTIVE-FRIENDLY PASSAGES

When might a passage call for an inductive-deductive sermon pattern? You might start out with an inductive outline, but as you work out how you are going to exposit the passage, you hit a point where you realize you need the inductive-deductive structure. *Any time a passage presents the full thesis somewhere in the middle, you are going to find that the inductive-deductive pattern is best.* Take Proverbs 9:7–12 for example. It begins by describing the scenarios in which the key difference between a wicked person and a righteous person is exposed. It gives examples of the difference, but it doesn't reveal the foundational difference right away. Then in verse 10 you get that key difference explicitly stated: "The fear of the LORD is the beginning of wisdom, and the knowledge of the Holy One is insight." This is the central thesis of the passage (if not the entire book) but it does not appear clearly until verse 10. Then the passage provides another couple of verses after verse 10 that further the wicked-righteous contrast. This is how inductive-deductive sermons work. You work *toward* the subject's complement and then, when you explicitly state it, you work *from* the complement the rest of the way. Many passages are laid out this way.

SUBJECT-COMPLETED-FRIENDLY PASSAGES

A passage of Scripture will point you to a subject-completed structure when it clearly presents multiple complements. There are at least a couple of ways Scripture does this. *First,* the biblical author may provide a list. We have a list in Matthew 28:19–20 where three participles describe how we are to make disciples (by going, by baptizing, and by teaching). We have qualifications for elders listed in Titus 1:5–9 or a list of instructions regarding the care of widows in 1 Timothy 5:3–16. These are the more obvious cases. A *second* way is when you discern there are two or more complements to the given subject. Let's say you are preparing a sermon on James 3:1–12 and you determine that there are at least two related but separate reasons as to why we must tame our tongues: we must tame them because an uncontrolled tongue can be destructive (vv. 5–8), and we must tame them because an uncontrolled tongue is incompatible with verbal worship (vv. 9–12). You are not approaching the text seeking to make it into a list. You are simply identifying that there is more than one complement to the author's single subject. What you want to avoid is pressing the subject-completed pattern onto texts that do not demand it. Not every text gives us "four ways" to do this, or "three steps" for doing that. But when the passage does truly provide more than one complement, go for the subject-completed approach.

CONCLUSION

For many, thinking in terms of sermon patterns will take some adjusting. But if you lend it your persistent attention, it will soon become natural to you. When you listen to preachers, ask yourself what pattern they are using.[74] Look over the past few sermons you have preached. Which of the four patterns discussed in this chapter best represent the structure you chose? Which do you gravitate toward? When you are reading a book, especially nonfiction, look at a paragraph or two and try to identify the general pattern. You can do this now. You will notice that above I used an inductive pattern to explain inductive-friendly passages: I began with a question and I did not answer the question completely in the next sentence. It took several sentences that progressively unfolded the answer so that by the last sentence you got the full thesis statement clearly stated. In fact, all of the paragraphs following that one employ the structure that they are describing.

When you are looking to structure your sermon to maximize tension, one of these four patterns will normally work. Over time you will be able to use others; there are more than four ways to structure a sermon and maintain tension. But to begin with, let these four structures master you. After some time, you will realize that you can combine them, alter them, and get creative. For example, you may come to passages at times where you

74. If you would like to see outlines of sermons I gave using each of the four structures, see Appendix C: Sample Sermon Outlines on page 201.

decide you want to use a different pattern than the one it seems to suggest. You might want to walk through certain passages in reverse order.[75] You might come upon a passage that is *chiastic* in its structure: the top and the bottom mirror each other and the punch of the passage is the middle portion. This is a marvelous literary device, but it does not translate well to oral discourse. If you preached chiastically, you would essentially preach your first half of the sermon again in your second half. There is no way to maintain tension at that point—there's nothing to anticipate! But you should feel the freedom to take the text out of order if it makes for a better communicative experience so long as the agenda of the text is honored. Make customizations once you feel you have mastered the four. For practice, take a look at Exercise 2: Practice Choosing Sermon Structures on page 169. Here you will be presented with passages and asked to choose a structure that would best fit. Suggested answers are provided with a brief explanation of the logic behind the choice.

Once you use an overarching question and a structure to develop the route that tension will take in your sermon, there is one more thing you need to do. If you walk your listeners through a text from problem to solution and stop there, you may still leave them without getting to what they really need. You need to get them to their *ultimate solution*.

---

75. John Piper did this for his sermon on Galatians 1 at the 2017 Gospel Coalition Conference (http://resources.thegospelcoalition.org/library/paul-s-pilgrimage-paul-s-plea from 12:05 to 15:28).

CHAPTER 4

Disclose the Ultimate Solution

Imagine going to a hospital that specializes in treating a disease that you recently discovered you have. You are devastated, but you know these doctors are top experts in the field. You go through a battery of tests, and the lead doctor finally sits you down to describe the disease to you in painstaking detail. You're getting all the bad news. But you know they have done their research, and you are hopeful they are going to give some good news. The doctor begins to show you pictures of what a healthy person looks like. Pictures of people smiling, laughing, playing sports, collaborating in the workplace, sleeping soundly at night. "This is what the disease-free life looks like," the doctor explains. Then he tells you to go home and be like the people in those pictures. He even sends you home with a portfolio of the pictures to look at. "Keep them as reminders of how to live," he urges. "Spend time looking intently at one of them each day to keep you going." Would you leave that office feeling hopeful? Is that doctor's advice worth listening to?

When we unpack a text of Scripture, we expose the disease in all of us. None of us lives like the text calls us to live. But if we send our listeners home without the specifically *Christian* context of the passage, we are simply asking them to go home, think about the verses intently, and live like they tell us to live. They can't. We can't. So the sermons are pointless and not worthy of being heard. We need perpetual doses of the only antidote that will enable us to live the way Scripture calls us to live. Not a one-time shot but a continued reliance on the only Source of grace and strength. If I explain a passage and tell my congregation to live like it says, their response should be similar to the way any of us might respond if we had a doctor give us pictures of healthy people rather than prescribing us the medicine. "I *try* to live like that, and sometimes I feel like I can pull it off for a day or two. But I can't keep it up; I just don't have the strength." This is the sad experience for many churchgoers. It is tiring and hopeless.

In a sermon, there is no point in presenting a problem and promising a solution if you do not provide a solution that works. Earlier we saw that exposition is what makes a sermon worthy of being heard, but sermonic exposition is incomplete without the context of the gospel. No matter the text, we need to point them to the ultimate solution in Jesus Christ. We need to get them to the good news. This is preaching that must be heard.

A THEOLOGY OF PREACHING THE ULTIMATE SOLUTION

When preaching a text—any text from anywhere in Scripture—we must point the listener to the ultimate solution in the gospel of Jesus Christ. Every time. This conviction stems from a biblical theology that sees the hope of Christ as the thematic unity of all of Scripture. I am not alone in believing this; there are many excellent books that detail this position masterfully and much more thoroughly than I can in this chapter.[76] Shortly, we will see how each sermon should ultimately resolve in the gospel of Jesus and what that looks like in relation to the thesis statement and maintaining tension. But first I want to set forth two reasons getting to the ultimate solution makes a sermon worthy of attention.

CHRIST IS THE CENTRAL OBJECT OF OUR FAITH

To understand the necessity of getting to the ultimate solution in every sermon, we need to understand the nature of faith and works. When the first Protestants sought reform in the Catholic Church, they drew a line in the sand regarding how we find right standing before God. They didn't like the Catholic math: grace *plus* works, humanity *plus* Christ, our righteousness *plus* his. When we look back at the stance the Reformers took, we often refer to them as the "solas." *Sola* (alone) is antithetical to the "plus" gospel. We are saved by grace alone, through faith alone, in Christ alone, to the glory of God alone. We know this because Scripture alone is our authority. Of course, faith and grace produce works. Genuine faith is shown in good works. But

76. For recent treatments, see for example: Vern S. Poythress, *Reading the Word of God in the Presence of God: A Handbook for Biblical Interpretation* (Wheaton, IL: Crossway, 2016, 220–302); Julius J. Kim, *Preaching the Whole Counsel of God: Design and Deliver Gospel-Centered Sermons* (Grand Rapids: Zondervan, 2015); Timothy Keller, *Preaching: Communicating Faith in an Age of Skepticism* (New York: Viking, 2015); and Dennis E. Johnson, *Him We Proclaim: Preaching Christ from All of Scripture* (Phillipsburg, NJ: P&R, 2007). Classic works include Edmund P. Clowney, *Preaching Christ in All of Scripture* (Wheaton, IL: Crossway, 2003); Graeme Goldsworthy, *Preaching the Whole Bible as Christian Scripture: The Application of Biblical Theology to Expository Preaching* (Grand Rapids: Eerdmans, 2000); Sidney Greidanus, *Preaching Christ from the Old Testament: A Contemporary Hermeneutical Method* (Grand Rapids: Eerdmans,1999); and Bryan Chapell, *Christ-Centered Preaching: Redeeming the Expository Sermon* (Grand Rapids: Baker, 1994, 2005).

faith and works do not cooperate to secure salvation. The work necessary to attain salvation is already provided in Christ *alone* (*solus Christus*). Then when a person is in Christ by faith alone, that faith does not remain alone—it is accompanied by works. Works won't get you to Jesus, but Jesus will get you to work. Yet human effort gets no credit in producing it (Eph 1:6, 12, 14, 19–20; 2:5–10). In other words, it is only by virtue of my faith in Christ that any works are produced in me.

Do not miss the import of this for preaching. If preachers reveal the tension in a passage but don't show how the *object* of the listener's faith must be Christ and not willpower, they're not directing their congregation to the real answer. It's like reading a captivating book that has built up amazing anticipation only to get to the end and see that there is no real resolution to the plot. Every sermon should get to Christ because every text reveals our need for grace, and we can only draw grace from Christ's work on our behalf. In his *Christologia,* John Owen explains, "It is evident that we can receive no good, no benefit, by virtue of any office of Christ, nor any fruits of their exercise, without an actual respect of faith unto his person, whence all their life and power is derived."[77] The whole of our faith is in Christ alone. A sermon has no benefit unless it calls our faith to cling to the person and work of Jesus Christ. The gospel is crucially necessary to every sermon.

If I preach a sermon from a text but I do not get the listener to Christ, what am I asking of them? Should they focus on their efforts? Their ability to do what the text demands? It is precisely a focus on their own ability that will fail them. We must urge our listeners at every pass to continually place their faith *in Christ*

---

77. John Owen and Andrew Thompson, *The Works of John Owen*, vol. 1, ed. William H. Goold (Edinburgh: T&T Clark, 1862), 85.

and not in their *faith* in Christ.[78] We need to get our listeners off of what Jerry Bridges called "the performance treadmill."[79] Christians need to understand that we are not saved by grace and then left to merit our own sanctification. We are justified by grace, sanctified by grace, and glorified by grace. Christ produces all of it, and the moment I think I can practice my discipleship apart from a perpetual placing of my faith wholly on Christ, I will fail. When introducing our listeners to the problem-solution in any passage, we must also point them to their ultimate solution in Christ lest they revert to our universal default setting of self-reliance.

CHRIST IS THE CENTRAL SUBJECT OF SCRIPTURE

Since Jesus is the central object of our faith, it makes sense that he is also the ultimate focus in all of Scripture. Consider Paul's reminder to the church at Corinth that while he was among them he preached nothing but Christ and him crucified (1 Cor. 2:2). According to Acts 18:11, Paul stayed with them at least eighteen months, perhaps longer (v. 18). Think about that. Paul stayed with the Corinthian church for at least a year and a half, and he could not be accused of ever preaching anything else except the person and redemptive work of Jesus Christ. What Scriptures did Paul use? The Old Testament.

This is not only a Paul thing. It's a Jesus thing. When Jesus walked with those two disciples toward Emmaus after his resurrection, he was not pleased with their inability to see the gospel in the Old Testament. So "beginning with Moses and all

---

78. As J. C. Ryle so helpfully explained in the chapter "Christ Is All" in his book *Holiness: Its Nature, Hindrances, Difficulties and Roots* (London: William Hunt and Company, 1889).

79. Jerry Bridges, *Transforming Grace: Living Confidently in God's Unfailing Love* (Colorado Springs: NavPress, 1991), 15–24.

the Prophets, he interpreted to them in all the Scriptures the things concerning himself" (Luke 24:27). Which Prophets? All of them. Which parts of Moses? All of it. Luke stressed it: "in all the Scriptures." If every major part of the Old Testament points to Christ, how can we preach even a subpart of it without reference to that crucial context? With every book of the Old Testament, Jesus took those disciples from their problem to the ultimate solution.

Jesus taught that he did not come to do away with the Law or the Prophets but to fulfill them. He came to accomplish them. How much of it did Jesus come to fulfill? Every iota, every dot (Matt 5:17–18). Jesus actually railed against teaching any of it apart from a focus on himself. He taught his critics that they could not combine their Jesus-less version of religion with the gospel. He taught that their religion was like a group of guests at a wedding feast fasting and mourning for a bridegroom (Mark 2:18–22). It makes no sense if the bridegroom for whom the feast is taking place is present. The gospel is different from their version of religion because the gospel is centered on Jesus. It recognizes the presence and identity of the bridegroom. Preaching an Old Testament passage without Jesus fits nicely with the theological framework of Christ's critics. But Jesus' opinion of such an understanding of things is that it cannot mesh with the gospel. The old wineskins won't do.

This means Jesus is never irrelevant to any Christian sermon. Never. Of course, he's the center of Scripture—he's the center of everything. Creation was mediated through Christ, meaning that life itself is Christ-centered (John 1:1–3). Our continued existence in this world is Christ-centered (Col 1). There are no blessings from God for which Christ is not central (Eph 1:3). Apart from Christ we can do nothing at all (John 15:5; Phil 4:13). I need to be in him to do anything and I need his strength in me to do all things. Where any Scripture demands that I do anything, I can only respond to that demand positively and successfully by faith in Christ. How can I leave that out of my sermon?

One might wonder why it is not enough that a sermon be simply *God* centered. Why specifically the Son? But to honor Christ *is* to honor God (John 17:1–2). To put it another way, honoring Christ is *how* God is honored (Rom 16:27; 1 Pet 4:11). Therefore, every sermon should honor God *by* honoring the Son. We honor the Son by pointing out to our listeners that he is the only and ultimate solution. That there is no other way to respond to the text than to follow its demands *by* fixing our faith continually on him. That, ultimately, we can only experience resolve in Christ. Every passage of Scripture moves us in this direction.

Do we see one sermon in the New Testament that leaves out the gospel?[80] Is there one epistle that does not center our hope on Christ or ground its demands in our faith in Christ? Why should the gospel be absent in our sermons? Any work demanded of us can only be accomplished as we "hold the faith in our Lord Jesus Christ" (Jas 2:1).

RESOLVING ANTICIPATION IN CHRIST

Christ-centered preaching has at times been misused. Not every passage necessarily reveals a type of Christ. Not every passage serves as an analogy. Preaching Christ does not mean that Jesus is to be injected into the text without regard to the original author's scope of revelation or immediate intent.

---

80. It has been argued that Paul's sermon to the "men of Athens" in Acts 17 is an example of a sermon that is not Christ-centered. If that is the case, verse 31 presents a problem: Who is the man God has appointed to judge the world? What was the circumstance of this man's resurrection? How did this resurrection provide assurance to those who repent? Of course, this sermon was gospel-centered. If it wasn't, these points would not make sense.

This is why in his commentaries Calvin would resist inserting New Testament revelation into the thinking of Old Testament writers. Rather, he would interpret those passages according to the light given those authors at the time, and in his sermons, he would mainly present the connection to Christ in the application portion.[81] But understand why he did this. He felt the weight of this obligation because we do not live before the incarnation; nevertheless, it would be "artificial and foolish" to preach those texts as if we were unaware of the further revelation—we must now preach "in a Christian way to Christian people."[82] How ironic that some view Christ-centered preaching of Old Testament passages as artificial. Indeed, it is sometimes done artificially. But for Calvin, it is *precisely* this christocentricity that makes the Old Testament relevant. He taught that we must preach the Old Testament, not just to clarify the background on some New Testament allusions, but because Christ is the fulfillment in the Old as he is in the New.[83]

Of course, not all evangelical preachers agree. In one of the more thoughtful rebuttals to Christ-centered preaching, Abraham Kuruvilla agrees that, according to the hermeneutical Rule of Centrality, the focus of our interpretation should be *the preeminent person of Christ and his redemptive work that fulfills the will of the Father in the power of the Holy Spirit*.[84] This interpretational focus is "for applicational purposes."[85] But he proposes *Christiconic* preaching over and against Christocentric

---

81. T. H. L. Parker, *Calvin's Preaching* (Louisville: Westminster John Knox, 1992), 92.

82. Ibid.

83. Ibid., 7.

84. Abraham Kuruvilla, *Privilege the Text! A Theological Hermeneutic for Preaching* (Chicago: Moody, 2013), 84; 238.

85. Ibid.

approaches. He believes that Christocentric approaches fail to do justice to the theology of the Old Testament text itself. The "Christiconic" preaching that he proposes seeks to keep Christ the focus of interpretation but without foisting Christ on every text. He wants to let each pericope simply say what it says, as it were, and trust that whatever comes from each passage will shape us into the *eikon* of Christ over time, "pericope by pericope."[86]

We can appreciate this attempt for its desire to agree with Christ-centered preachers that Christ should be central to our interpretation. We should also appreciate the goal of protecting the local meaning of any text. Too often, preachers jump straight to Jesus, making the text almost marginal to the point. The sermon could have been preached from any text because the immediate agenda of the text is sidelined to get to the gospel. This is not what I am commending here. Yet the absence of an explicit mention of the person and work of Christ in the sermon runs contrary to the ministry of the word as modeled in the New Testament, as we have seen. Preaching Christ should not mean that the immediate situation in the text is ignored. As Sidney Greidanus has explained, the problem is when we draw a straight line from the saints in the text to application for our lives. Instead, we must understand what God is doing in and through those persons in the text.[87] And what God is doing is pointing us to Christ.

What had long been a mystery is now given to us in Jesus. The mystery that is revealed is the gospel—that God himself strengthens us according to Christ and that we are now able

86. Ibid., 262.

87. Sidney Greidanus, *Sola Scriptura: Problems and Principles in Preaching Historical Texts* (Toronto: Wedge Publishing, 1970), 146–47.

to live lives of obedience through faith in Christ specifically (Rom 16:25–26). Why would we preach as if the gospel were still shrouded in mystery? Why preach an Old Testament text as if we were Old Testament saints? We have the revelation of Jesus Christ and we dare not leave it out in an attempt to respect the situation of the original audience. That would be to the detriment of *your* audience. And that would be to rebuff the gospel of Jesus Christ, whom we must proclaim. There is no other way to present anyone mature before God (Col 1:28). We must resolve every problem raised by every text through the specifics of the text—and ultimately in Christ.

Another criticism of Christ-centered preaching is that it is a monotonous approach—it is boring to provide the answer "Jesus" each week.[88] But where else is the answer located if not in our union with Christ? Yes, the Christ-centered preacher should use the details of each text and do truthfully. But there is nothing boring about the gospel. It is life and hope, strength and nutriment. What's more, we should not develop a theology or practice of preaching based on questions about what is exciting. We bear a responsibility to clarify the old mystery. To demonstrate how hearts of flesh can now respond to God's teaching in Scripture. We show how the gospel enlivens us and keeps us so that we can live the exciting details of every text. What is more disheartening than hearing sermons over and over again that burden us with dos and don'ts that we cannot maintain? There is nothing boring about accessing the same antidote again and again if that is the only way to keep us from suffering a myriad of diseases.

Or perhaps some might dismiss preaching Christ in every sermon because it is too depressing to always expose a problem.

---

88. Carl R. Trueman, *The Wages of Spin: Critical Writings on Historic & Contemporary Evangelicalism* (Fearn, Scotland: Christian Focus Publications, 2004), 172.

Who wants to suffer the conviction of utter failure in every sermon before getting to the "good news"? But the focus is not on despair; it is on the relief of grace in Christ. Without the mediatory work of Christ, we cannot approach God, please God, or glorify God. If a sermon calls the listener to approach God, please God, or glorify God, then it must provide the way to do so—by continually setting our faith on Christ alone. That is not a message of despair; that is a message of hope.

The truth is that people are already in despair. Their marriages need help. Their kids are difficult. Their jobs are sources of great anxiety. Culture creates a pressure to look a certain way, have certain things. Every text exposes some aspect of *why* they struggle or why they *should* struggle if they were previously unaware of the predicament. Preachers are not creating a problem; we are seeing in the text a problem that we already universally share. Then we point them to the answer. The text equips people, and Christ empowers them to use this equipping in their lives. The power to respond to the text resides not in the text but in Christ. And when we capture the movement from problem to solution to ultimate solution in the text, attention will perk.

PREACHING THE GOSPEL FROM EVERY PASSAGE

There are at least two dangers to avoid when preaching Christ from any text. The first is *missing* the text—failing to honor the details of the passage we are preaching. Exposition is lost. The second is to *misuse* the details of the text in order to get to Christ. We will cover these in order.

DON'T MISS THE TEXT

As a general rule, I favor the approach of leaving the connection to Christ for the end of the sermon. This is not a hard-and-fast rule. But it is a good habit to get the details of the text out there first, explained and clarified, sometimes even applied along the way. You teach what the text means, and you teach what it means for your audience in practical terms. Application can be as you go or bunched at the end.[89] But for me the connection to the gospel will normally come after all of that because it gives the power to live out what was just explained. We don't want to rush to get to Christ. The particulars in the text are inspired for our profit. We must demonstrate how the details are important in order to understand the thrust of the text. We move from details to overall meaning to application. This is moving from problem to solution. The anticipation that builds is a longing for the answer: how this text is going to show us what to do (or not do) or believe (or not believe) about this particular subject. That is helpful and profitable. But remember that we cannot do or believe anything righteous apart from Christ. Christians need the gospel again and again or else we will lean on our own strength to accomplish the demands of any text. So we move from details to overall meaning to application to empowerment. Problem to solution to ultimate solution.

Imagine you are preaching Genesis 4:1–16, the passage where we read of the rift between God and Cain. The text begins by contrasting the two brothers, Cain and Abel. Abel's sacrifice is accepted, Cain's is not. In comparisons, differences speak loudly. The clue to finding the problem with Cain's offering is in the description of Abel's—he brought the *first*born of his flock and their *fat* portions. Cain is enraged. He seems to think God is unreasonable, unfair. Perhaps he thinks God is arrogant or selfish. We notice, however, that God does not make this about

---

89. The rule for application to remember is that you must only apply universal truths universally. Because something is true in the text for the original audience does not mean it transfers to today's audience.

himself in the conversation. God has every right to demand worship, but he takes a different tack.

He warns Cain for his own good. Sin wants to have mastery over Cain, but he must gain mastery over it. Cain does not heed the warning and he murders his brother. We expect God to really pounce on him, and he does, but not with vengeance. God does explain to Cain that Abel's blood calls out to him—God is just and he cannot leave a deficit of justice ignored. But God does not match the punishment to the crime. He does not extinguish Cain. He expels him. Cain, having been shown this mercy, still has the nerve to object! Expulsion is too much to bear, he complains, because he will be in danger with others seeking vengeance. God says he will protect Cain by marking him in a way that will communicate to others that if Cain is killed, vengeance will be taken on the guilty party sevenfold. Cain suffers consequences but God stays his hand. Not only does he relent from the full brunt of vengeance that Cain deserves, but he teaches Cain about the nature of sin and he protects him in his exile.

What about this man merits God's patience and care? We see here a worsening of sin in the world from one generation to the next. There is a pattern—man sins and God comes asking questions. Adam and Eve shifted blame, but Cain is sarcastic in his refusal to acknowledge his wrongdoing. Eve had to be convinced to sin by the serpent, but Cain wouldn't be convinced *not* to sin by God himself. It is amazing how God responds—if anyone deserved to be struck dead, it's Cain. He ends up leading an entire city of rebellious people. No repentance, no remorse. God shows mercy in the face of persistent spite. The star of this passage is not Abel; it's God.

These details are important for establishing the primary truth revealed about God in this passage. As we prepare a sermon, we think about what this passage communicates about God that transfers across time and culture. The problem addressed is our view of God and his requirement to be worshipped and put first. The subject can be stated like this: *Why does God demand worship from us?* We might think God is harsh and sets up rules to make things difficult, but he is gracious and reveals to us what will go well for us and what will master us if we let it. We all have debt that cries out to God. All sins deserve death (Rom 6:23). But God is gracious in not only allowing our worship of him but in explaining to us that our worship is not only for his glory but also for our good. The solution that the text provides is to demonstrate the incredible, longsuffering love of God toward us even when we are rebellious and ugly. The answer is that *God requires worship because he cares for us.*

So far you are ready to take your listeners to the text and expose the problem in all of us—we can find it difficult to worship God and give him absolute primacy in our lives when we have a poor view of him. You are also ready to walk them through the particulars of the passage to point them to the answer: God is an amazingly gracious God who not only demands worship, but guides it and tells us how to protect it. It will go well with us to put God first and resist the sinful temptation to downgrade God's primacy in our lives. You are ready to move your listeners from problem to solution. But if you leave the sermon here, what do your listeners go home with? An impossible task. What they hear is, "You should recognize that God requires primacy in your life for his glory, yes, but also for your own good. Go home and make him first and you will see how things will go well with you. You will experience God's favor in the good times and the bad, in the ups and the downs. Put him first and you will see how fulfilling it is to walk with God and in his good pleasure." Their response will be to "try" to do that. But their faith needs to be set on Christ in order to do it.

Sin is crouching at the door for us too. It wants to master us and it often does. What power do I have to rule over sin? We know the answer. It is to live *with* Christ (Rom 6:8). To be dead to sin is to be alive to God *in* Christ Jesus (v. 6:11). It is our being with and in Christ that results in sin having no more dominion over us (v. 6:14). The only way to not be dominated by sin is to have our faith persist in Christ. We cannot leave this out.

A sermon on Genesis 4:1–16, then, must at least end with a reminder of the gospel. We are not to simply go home and think better of God and his intentions. We can't just put God first more often, more thoroughly. Rather, the sermon should remind listeners that we cling to Christ *in order* to live like that. We can't put off any evil if we don't consciously put on Christ and his armor of light (Rom 13:12–14). How does the Christian resist the flesh, make no provision for it, refuse to gratify its desires? How does the Christian resist the sin crouching at the door? There's only one way: continually put on Christ. We as preachers ask our listeners to be unlike Cain and understand the true character of God by pointing them to the cross. The cross is the supreme demonstration of God's love for us even while we were yet sinners like Cain (Rom 5:8). What does it mean that when we put God first in our lives that things will go well for us? The answer is in the gospel. It doesn't mean that nothing bad will happen. It means that all the good and bad things that happen are orchestrated by God to an ultimate end, which is the conformity to Jesus Christ available to those who are justified in him (Rom 8:28–29). If we don't get our listeners to the particulars of the text, we miss what the gospel is the ultimate answer *to*. But if we don't get our listeners to the gospel, we leave them with an immediate answer that they are likely to struggle in their own strength to apply.

Ironically, we can just as easily miss the good news in a New Testament passage. We can be in a Gospel and miss the gospel. In Luke 6:27–36, Jesus teaches us to be merciful even to those who are unmerciful toward us. A sermon can simply explain that the passage teaches us to be merciful and that God grieves at our lack of mercy because we would be behaving so unlike him. But if we do not focus the faith of our listeners on Christ, we are not helping them resist the temptation to revert to striving in the flesh. Instead, we must remind them that Jesus did not teach in a vacuum. He taught on his way to the cross, which would make obedience possible.

We can easily slip into preaching law in New Testament passages. Be holy (1 Pet 1:15–16), be joyful (Phil 4:4), pray at all times (Eph 6:18), forgive (Eph 4:32). When these verses are preached outside the context of the gospel, we are sending our listeners home with tasks to accomplish without reminding them that it is their faith in Christ alone that can produce results. In order to get them to a solution that works, we must explain what the solution looks like—we're like the doctors that show pictures of healthy people to our patients, except we also write the prescription for the serum that can change them. We get them to the ultimate solution of the gospel of Jesus Christ.

When you do this, you are exposing a deeper layer of the tension that you have already introduced. When you spotlight the problem, you capitalize on the listeners' anticipation of the solution. But as you're unpacking the solution, more mature Christians might realize that they cannot live this way. Some of your listeners might be feeling the weight of the reality awaiting them—they've tried and tried before but change is hard. This is a different layer of tension, and you can even make it explicit with a few short sentences. Rub it in a little. Then point them to the ultimate solution in the gospel. Every time.

DON'T MISUSE THE TEXT

The other way preachers can go awry in trying to preach Christ from every text is to think that they must discover some analogy or type in the passage in order to get to Christ. I think this is more common than many preachers allow in their exposition of Old Testament passages. But it is not always true that a passage contains some kind of foreshadowing of Jesus. We want to expose our listeners' need for the ultimate solution, but we want to do it responsibly. Every Old Testament text points to our need for the gospel, but they don't all do it in the same way.

Some Old Testament passages point us to the gospel by simply taking their place in a long historical process of the unfolding plan of redemption. There is not necessarily an analogy or type, just a notch in the successive revealing of God's redemption plan that points forward to Christ. What the Old Testament saints understood in part, we understand more fully. We can explain the text in its historical setting, but then we need to see how it projects forward into a fuller revelation in the gospel. Vern Poythress uses a helpful illustration on this point:

> Suppose an earthly father teaches his son John 3:16 and explains its meaning. Suppose the son grows up, and even goes to seminary to study the Bible more deeply. The son then recalls at one point how his father, years ago, first taught him about John 3:16. What did the father intend to convey? He intended that the son would understand John 3:16 in a way that a child is capable of. But he also intended that the son would continue to return to the verse, and would understand more and more as time passed. He intended that the boy's understanding would grow. So the father's intention encompassed the earlier

> understanding, the growth, and the later understanding, all in one unified purpose.[90]

God's plan of redemption becomes clearer over the course of revelation. So we can dig into an Old Testament text, explain what it demands of us, how it profits us and equips us, but then we move forward out of the mystery and into the more complete revelation of the gospel. The gospel shows how faith operates by its being set specifically on Christ, the fulfillment of all Scripture. We could preach the text as if we did not know the fuller scope of revelation and the gospel, but this would be to preach as the child and not as the seminary graduate. To use another of Poythress's illustrations, this would be to keep the picture of God's redemption plan for us unnecessarily blurry when it has been brought into focus for us in the gospel.[91] So some of your sermons will resolve the deeper layer of tension by bringing what is blurry in the Old Testament text into focus in Jesus Christ. Because of the gospel, we know the power to really live this passage.

All Old Testament texts take their place in the progress of revelation by serving as a rudimentary explanation of what will later be clarified. It is true that sometimes they do this by way of analogy or type/symbolism, but we should never force it onto a text that doesn't beg for it. Certainly, when a New Testament author gives it to us, we *must* see it there and explain it. It doesn't matter whether we see a type of Jesus in Jonah; Jesus did (Matt 12:39–41). It is also difficult to ignore the obvious parallels between Jonah and Jesus. Both are commissioned by God to preach repentance—Jonah reluctantly, Jesus sacrificially.

---

90. Poythress, *Reading the Word of God in the Presence of God* (Wheaton, IL: Crossway, 2016), 227–28.

91. Ibid., 228.

Both are on a boat in the middle of a storm that is threatening the lives of everyone on board. Both are fast asleep below deck. Both are awakened by panicked seamen, distraught and incredulous that one among them might be asleep and not helping. The sea is calmed by God when Jonah is thrown into it. The sea is calmed by Jesus because he is Lord over it. Jonah's episode ends with a response of fear and sacrifice from the pagan sailors. Jesus' episode ends with the disciples' fear and evolving faith (Jonah 1:1–16; Matt 8:23–27; Mark 4:35–41; Luke 8:22–25). Jonah blocks judgment by going into the judgement himself. When he comes out alive, he leads many into repentance and worship of God. Jesus blocks judgment by going into death itself. He comes out of the tomb alive and spreads the kingdom of God through his disciples leading many into repentance and worship of God.

Sometimes we do not have an overt connection made for us by a New Testament author, but parallels are hard to ignore. We don't see the New Testament draw parallels from the account of Abraham being called to sacrifice his son Isaac in Genesis 22 in any explicit way. But it is difficult not to see it: the one and only son born by divine intervention and according to divine promise; the willing and innocent son who carries the wood of the sacrifice up a slope in order to *be* the sacrifice; a willing father trusting that his son will be resurrected; God stopping it, explaining that what he really wants is faith, fear, obedience, and saying that he will provide the sacrifice to which faith is applied. We must preach Christ from Genesis 22. We are not to respond to this passage by placing faith in our own sacrifices. A sermon about sacrificing more for God would miss the point. God *stops* the sacrifice and commends Abraham for his fear and obedience. But the sacrifice is God's. We must fear and obey, but we obey *in the context* of God's provisional sacrifice.

But again, we must be careful. Not every mention of wood in the Old Testament necessitates a connection to the cross. The color scarlet does not require a connection to the blood of Christ. If your listeners walk away from the sermon thinking they would *never* be able to make that connection, you probably imposed it. If they walk away understanding that, in time and with diligent study, they would have been able to see that connection—that it is obvious once the overwhelming evidence is presented—then you are on the right track. We must avoid any temptation to become overly fixated on "discovering" types and analogies. When they are obvious, use them to describe the gospel. But whether the text operates typologically or not, we must fix our listeners' faith on Christ and his power to change us.

The point of calling attention to these kinds of connections is not simply to see how interesting they are, but to point to the empowering gospel of Jesus. In our sermon on Genesis 4:1–16, we may see Abel as somehow connecting to Jesus. Jesus is also killed as an innocent man who was pleasing to God, who enjoyed God's favor. But Jesus' blood doesn't cry out for judgment; it takes the judgment for us. Thus, Jesus' blood speaks a better word than Abel's (Heb 12:24). So here we can use Abel and his death as a pointer toward Jesus' death. But Jesus' death brings into better focus how God handles justice and how he is able to apply forgiveness to those who have blood on their hands but repent. We also saw the shedding of blood when God made skins for Adam and Eve just a few verses earlier. Something had to die in order to cover them. This is not a full-blown rollout of the sacrificial system, but it is an introduction to the concept. The system brings it into greater focus, but the gospel reveals it in full detail. Then of course we have Genesis 3:15 in close proximity, promising in seminal form the coming Savior. I believe this verse pushes into all of Scripture, but surely it looms over Genesis 4.

We don't get the listener to the gospel artificially. We make the connections *from* the text. In this case, we can see that Jesus' blood provides the forgiveness we need because we have failed like Cain. Jesus' blood provides the grace we need to make us into the worshippers we need to be. Jesus is the serpent crusher to whom we must look for strength in our battle against sin.

Whichever way we see the connection to the gospel from an Old Testament passage, we must understand that stopping at the blurry solution that the Old Testament provides is not enough. We need to show our listeners the clearer picture of God's grace in the gospel. Not only does this portion of the sermon deepen the tension, but it provides the ultimate solution.

THE ULTIMATE SOLUTION AND THE THESIS STATEMENT

When I write a thesis statement for a sermon, sometimes the connection to Christ is explicit in the statement itself. Other times it is not. For example, in a sermon on Exodus 1:1–2:10, my thesis statement was: *We should fear God more than man because God always gets his way.* The sermon gets to the ultimate solution in Christ, but it doesn't appear in the thesis statement. Most of my theses throughout my sermon series on Exodus looked like this.[92] But some expressed the ultimate solution. My thesis for verses 24:12–31:18 was: *We can be assured of our relationship with God because Jesus is our perfect priest.* There's no need to make a hard-and-fast rule here about whether to include the ultimate solution in the thesis statement. But there is a general principle I try to follow.

If the text itself points to Christ in some obvious way, I will likely include the ultimate solution in the thesis statement.

---

92. To see all my thesis statements, structures, and overarching questions for that series, see Appendix B: Sample Map of a Sermon Series on Exodus on page 183.

Since the thesis statement is an encapsulation of what the text itself is driving at, it makes sense to include the Christ connection that is evident in the passage. But if the connection is not clear from the text, then I tend to leave it out of the thesis statement. I let the text speak for itself—its own problem and solution. But of course in the sermon, I *apply* the thesis statement in the context of the gospel. If the text doesn't get to the gospel by symbolism or type, then I will explain that this passage is on a trajectory toward greater clarification in the gospel of Jesus Christ and I will teach that the only way to effectively respond to the call of these verses is to focus our faith on Christ.

CONCLUSION

You've probably heard the phrase a thousand times: "Give a man a fish and you feed him for a day. Teach a man to fish and you feed him for a lifetime." The same idea applies here: "Give a man a text and you might feed him for a day. Teach him Christ and you feed him for a lifetime."

We cannot give our listeners pieces of text and not show them how to live it in Christ's strength. They might be able to go home and apply the passage to their lives for a day or two on their own energy. But it will fail them. Apart from a clear exhortation to lean on Christ, we lead our listeners from problem to solution to another problem. We reveal tension only to leave it unresolved. But if we continue to teach reliance on Jesus, we lead them from problem to solution to ultimate solution. Only the gospel can truly resolve any tension.

Don't leave your people hanging. Don't send them home with portraits of healthy saints to look at. Send them home with a fixation on Christ. Give them the prescription of the gospel. But even if you do this, if your sermon does not grab them from the beginning, they may not lend their attention long enough to get them to the gospel. That's why writing a compelling introduction is crucial.

CHAPTER 5

Introducing Tension

In my house, movies have to pass our twenty-minute rule. The rule was created one night when my wife wasn't very excited about a movie I wanted to try and I offered a compromise: "Let's give it twenty minutes—if it doesn't interest us by then, we'll turn it off." Since then it's become habit. If a movie does not hook us within the first twenty minutes, we're not going to waste the next hour and a half hoping that it eventually gets good. Preacher, every listener before you has a similar rule.

It is a commonly shared truth that a speaker has a very short window of time before the listener decides he or she is just not interested—and then they'll tune you out. You don't have anywhere near twenty minutes, either. Bryan Chapell finds the estimate to be about thirty seconds.[93] When you have people sitting before you, each with a conscious or subconscious "thirty-second rule," you do not have time to make your introduction about anything else but generating tension.

The introduction to the sermon is crucial to developing tension. It is a crucial piece that makes the most sense to write once

93. Bryan Chapell, *Christ-Centered Preaching: Redeeming the Expository Sermon*, 2nd ed. (Grand Rapids: Baker, 2005), 239.

the other tension elements have been considered. As we have covered, the expository preacher can generate tension by:

> First, discovering the problem-solution heart of the passage and expressing it in one clear thesis statement;
>
> second, identifying the point of tension and expressing it in the overarching question; and
>
> third, determining which structure would best carry tension for the particular text of Scripture.

The overarching question that comes out of the thesis will carry the tension throughout the sermon until the end. The preacher would be remiss, however, not to think critically about the introduction to the sermon. It needs to grab the listener quickly. The introduction starts the engine. It brings out the problem that the passage is going to address and help us with. It is the time where you convince the audience they need to listen. To this point, you have prepared by writing your thesis statement, your overarching question, and your structure. Now you can work on the introduction because you know what you're introducing. As the preacher, *you* know where you're going and why, but the listeners don't. Without an effective introduction they will not follow you eagerly into the text. In this chapter, I will begin by telling you the primary function of the sermon's introduction, then let you know how the introduction can set up tension for the body of the sermon.

GENERATING TENSION BY REVEALING THE NEED

Tension is birthed at the revealing of a need. For the preacher concerned with winning attention, the introduction is not merely a prelude to information. It is setting the table for the tension that will be resolved by the text of Scripture. As expository preachers, we don't set the text aside to address what we think the listener's questions are. Instead, we need to convince them that they have questions that this text answers. The introduction must communicate why the text must be given attention. Your audience may not have walked in understanding why they need this Scripture passage, but after your introduction they should. Rather than assuming your listeners understand their need for the passage, you must show them why they personally need it—why they should be concerned with this text. And this must happen *before* the text is exposited. When describing David Cook's preaching effectiveness, Simon Vibert notes that he "actively seeks to enter the world of the listener before assuming that the listener will enter into the world of his sermon."[94] The preacher does this by revealing a need.

Revealing the need captures interest. There are many variables when it comes to what impedes a listener's attention. Emotional barriers, poor listening skills, mental or physical distractions—to name a few. But the element that is most in the speaker's control is gaining the listeners' attention by piquing interest. The listeners will decide whether they will listen almost right on contact. And we can do something about that. Pierre Marcel, author of *The Relevance of Preaching,* put it wisely: "Believers must know that the preached word, to be relevant, must be drawn from Scripture."[95] He continued: "What, then, is the first condition of *the relevance* of the *preached* word? It is that this preaching be drawn from the ever relevant revelation

94. Simon Vibert, *Excellence in Preaching: Studying the Craft of Leading Preachers* (Downers Grove, IL: InterVarsity Press, 2011), 81.

95. Pierre Ch. Marcel, *The Relevance of Preaching*, trans. Rob Roy McGregor (Grand Rapids: Baker, 1963), 58.

of the Holy Scripture."[96] Scripture is both how we *win* attention and that to which we *point* attention.

THE NEED FOR THE TEXT

If the introduction fails to focus sharply on a need, not only will holding interest prove difficult, but the purpose of preaching itself will have been neglected. The ultimate purpose of preaching is to bring glory to God, but the means to that end is bringing people to reckon with their deep need for grace. Every passage meets some need by equipping us where we were formerly ill-equipped or incomplete (2 Tim 3:17). This is not one of many purposes for the sermon. It is *the* purpose.

Bryan Chapell has stated that it is not enough to determine the subject of a passage. We must determine its purpose. He calls this the *Fallen Condition Focus* of the passage:

> The Fallen Condition Focus (FCF) is the mutual human condition that contemporary believers share with those to or about whom the text was written that requires the grace of the passage for God's people to glorify and enjoy him. ... Because an FCF is a human problem or burden addressed by specific aspects of a scriptural text, informed preaching strives to unveil this purpose in order to explain each passage properly.[97]

Thus, we reveal the need that is rooted in the passage. This immediately generates tension because the spiritual deficit that requires grace is a problem that needs solving. And this should be brought out right in the introduction.

---

96. Ibid.

97. Chapell, *Christ-Centered Preaching*, 50.

In order to generate tension, you must make the overarching question unmistakably clear *in the introduction*. The very purpose of the introduction is to bring the audience to that question. The overarching question works because the introduction convinces listeners that they need the answer. They embark on an investigative quest, like a mystery. In his book on nonfiction writing, Philip Gerard discusses the nature of mystery: "Mystery is not just what we don't know; it's what we don't know *and really want to know*. Mystery is any unanswered question that piques our curiosity."[98] What keeps a reader turning pages in a novel is what keeps a listener hanging in with the preacher at every turn—a burning question. Introductions are necessary because it is not enough to present a question. You must persuade your audience that it is *their* question—that they want to know the answer and the answer is in this passage. You already know why they need this text. You need to help *them* understand why, and you need to do that right away. But oftentimes we delay this work or confuse it because our introductions are divided.

AN UNDIVIDED INTRODUCTION

Homileticians will tell you that the purpose of the introduction is to gain your listeners' interest and to focus their attention on the subject of the sermon.[99] Two essential functions. But these should not be viewed as two separate halves of the introduction. The idea is not to command attention and *then* reveal the need. More effectively, we should command attention *by* revealing the

98. Philip Gerard, *Creative Nonfiction: Researching and Crafting Stories of Real Life* (Cincinnati: Story Press, 1996), 166 (italics his).

99. See for example Haddon Robinson, *Biblical Preaching*, 166–67; Bryan Chapell, *Christ-Centered Preaching*, 238–40; Donald Sunukjian, *Invitation to Biblical Preaching*, 192.

need. You capture attention *with* the need. This has the potential to really streamline and focus your introduction.

You can start your sermon with an intriguing quote or gripping story—but you don't have to. These things will most likely command attention and you will use them to reveal the need, but they are not intrinsic to a good introduction. You can cut straight to the chase. You might find it effective to introduce the need in your opening sentence:

> "If you were asked why you read your Bible, what would be your very first response?"
>
> "How can God expect me to forgive someone for something that I can never forget?"
>
> "Here's a truth most of us probably rarely consider: if we partake in the Lord's Supper without examining ourselves, we eat and drink judgment on ourselves."
>
> "While we often equate death with utter loss, the Bible teaches that, for Christians, death is incomparable *gain*."

The need can come in the first sentence or the second or the third—the point is there does not have to be a paragraph or two of gaining attention and *then* a paragraph or two on our need for the text. There will be times where you can just get right to it in the opening lines. A story or powerful quotation is great when it really helps. But we shouldn't start writing our introductions by asking, "What great story can I capture their attention with for this sermon?" The question should be, "How can I get them to understand why they need Scripture to address this need?" Sometimes you will think of a really effective analogy, a set of surprising statistics or a recent example from your own life. But telling an engrossing story is not the point; generating tension via the need is.

The introduction for a sermon I preached on Philippians 4:4–7 went something like this:

> In bookstores all over, there's no shortage of titles like *How to Find Joy*. Maybe at home if you look on your nightstand or your bookshelf you might see a title that looks something like *Seven Steps to Greater Happiness*. These books are how-to books—how to *find* joy, how to *discover* joy. But what I submit to you is that joy—no matter how much you strive for it, no matter how many steps you try to take to reach it—cannot be *found*. You can't find joy, and the reason you can't find joy is that joy is not something you *find*. Joy is something you *do*.

The need I'm hitting on is our universal desire for a joy and happiness that we can't seem to get. It's a problem because while we desire it, we're going about it the wrong way. My intention is to get my listeners to rethink their entire conception of what joy in the Christian life looks like. To take what they view as a noun that they must have and cast it as a verb that they must do. My hope was that even the veteran Christians in the room might wonder where I was going with this. The obvious question in light of this introduction is, "How do you *do* joy?" I wanted to get them ready for the text and, in this one example, it took about forty seconds to do it. Many introductions will be considerably longer. But they don't have to be long. Your introduction needs to be as long as it takes to get your audience sensing their need for the text.

Most folks will turn to the text if you simply ask them. But the introduction functions to get the audience *hungry* for the text. To *want* to turn to it. If they didn't bring a Bible to church that day, you want them to wish they did. By revealing the need you generate a sense of anticipation and expectation—tension.

When they understand that the text is going to resolve that tension for them, they are given much more incentive to turn there in their Bibles and stay with you as you walk them through it. Yet the transition from the introduction to the reading of the text is a difficult move. We need to think carefully about how we segue from the introduction to the passage.

THE SEGUE TO THE PASSAGE

Even in a sermon where the introduction is handled well, tension can be fumbled in transit to the first verse of the Bible passage. A track athlete may run a record-breaking first lap of a relay race and the next runner may possess amazing potential, but the baton can still be dropped on the transfer. In a sermon, tension must be transferred carefully from the introduction to the exposition of the text.

Since you have just prompted the overarching question in the introduction, you will want to connect the question to the text quickly. This is easier said than done. Often, the text does not immediately address the question that has been raised. The passage will eventually answer the question, but it will not always be right away. The danger is when the preacher promises the answer is in the text and the audience does not see the answer in the first verse. This dissipates tension.

To begin with, preachers should explain to their listeners the background of the original audience and how that audience shared a need with them. Again, the best way to segue to the text, without losing the need-based tension, is to explain why the *original* audience needed this passage. Not only does this give the listeners the appropriate backdrop to the passage; it also helps them understand why the passage begins the way it does.

Let's look at a sample introduction to an inductive sermon on 2 Peter 3:1–13 that does *not* do this well:

> Over 2,000 years ago Jesus and his disciples taught that he would return in power and glory. For centuries—millennia—Christians have been awaiting Christ's return. We don't want to doubt, but as the world seems to worsen, it just seems like it's been so long. Is he coming back? Why has he taken this long? How much longer can he take? Aren't we a laughingstock in the world, clinging to the promise of a Messiah who said he'd return? *Why hasn't Jesus returned yet?* (overarching question)
>
> <In today's text we're going to find the answer. Turn to 2 Peter chapter 3. > Let's look at verse 1 ...

This introduction sets up the overarching question well, but it fails to set up the passage. The segue from the intro to the text is marked by the angle brackets, <... >. It's too brief and doesn't pass the baton. The listener is expecting an answer to the question but won't really get it until verse 9 (the repentance of sinners who have not yet come). The audience is going to read verse 1 and not see the answer. They are going to wonder what happened to the overarching question.

A better way to segue to the passage might look like this:

> <In today's text we're going to find the answer. Turn to 2 Peter chapter 3. Here we're going to see that Peter's audience wrestles with the same question. They are losing heart because they are experiencing an increasingly hostile world toward Christianity and they are discouraged that Jesus isn't back yet. In fact, they are surrounded by scoffers who mock them for waiting. *Why hasn't Jesus returned?* Peter begins by reminding them that their very expectation is based on authoritative prophecy—not wishful thinking or some fairy tale. This expectation is real.>
>
> Let's look at verse 1 ...

In this example, the preacher takes a few more seconds to orient the audience to what is going on in the passage—why Peter is writing this and to whom. The preacher is underscoring the tension that has been raised by showing that the original audience experienced a similar tension. This is why this passage was born. Then the preacher explains that the first verse is going somewhere.[100] It does not answer the overarching question, but it begins setting the table for the answer. The expectation of the return of Christ is not one that should be given up. The preacher is implying that the answer to the overarching question is ahead, but what verse 1 addresses must be discussed first. This keeps the tension intact as the listener journeys through the passage toward the answer.

We can apply this same strategy to preaching in the deductive structure. Here the preacher makes a statement that prompts listeners to think of their own questions (questions that demand proof or explanation). This usually makes a smoother transition to the text of Scripture because the first verses will normally provide a natural response even if it is not the whole response. But the segue still needs to involve a connection between the shared need of the original audience and today's listeners. For example, a deductive sermon on Romans 13:1–7 might begin like this:

> Well, the votes are in. We have a new president. Now some of you might be rejoicing. Others of you, well, you're having a hard time. Elections and inaugurations are always a difficult time for Christians, aren't they? Many of us feel like we are left deciding to vote for the lesser of evils. We live in this world yet we belong to a greater kingdom. And when the authorities of this world

---

100. Sunukjian calls this a "preview" and he explains it well in *Invitation to Biblical Preaching*. 221–23.

differ from the values of our King, we struggle. Why should we support them? Why pay taxes to them? Maybe I can lie on my tax forms and justify it by taking what I save and donating it to a pro-life cause. But the Bible is clear on this with an emphatic "No." *We must submit ourselves to our governing authorities, totally.* Regardless of who they are, whether or not they are Christian. *We must submit ourselves to our governing authorities, totally.* (Implicit overarching question: "Really? Can you prove that?" Or "Explain that to me, how is that so?")

<In today's passage Paul tells the Christians in Rome to do exactly that. Keep in mind that the Roman Empire was *particularly* depraved. Yet Paul still gives them this command in verse 1 ...>

In this case the preacher is still showing how the original audience shared the same need, but there is less in the way of previewing what that first verse is going to say. This is because in a deductive sermon the first verse or verses normally reveal the complement quite directly. In either case, whether using the inductive or deductive approach, the preacher will want to make sure the introduction segues to the text without losing tension. The way to ensure this is to introduce the text by explaining how the author is addressing the same need with the original audience.

I sometimes use another way to introduce the text when it is a notoriously difficult passage to interpret. Whether it is historically a centerpiece to major theological debates or it is a cryptic parable or otherwise strange text, I sometimes use that as my "hook." Even for those in the audience who are not familiar with the text or that it is widely known for being difficult, this approach at least gives them the early caution that this is going to be an especially tough nut to crack but that we admit it and we are going to do it together. If the passage is so hard that it is going to take time to even establish the *subject*, let alone the complement, you might want to consider this approach.

Introductions are a joy to write, and it is rewarding to see faces locked in with you when you ask them to turn to a passage. But no introduction is complete without a conclusion.

CONCERNING THE CONCLUSION

Why include a section on conclusions in a chapter about introductions? Because your conclusion has everything to do with your introduction. If you understand the power of an overarching question. then you understand why the introduction needs to set the question up. It's the purpose of the introduction. But the purpose of the conclusion is to clarify the answer. The conclusion needs to provide in no uncertain terms the answer to the overarching question.

This becomes even more crucial in a sermon following an inductive pattern. Since in the inductive sermon the listeners do not get the answer until the very end, they need as clear and repeated an explanation of the entire thesis statement in the conclusion as you can muster. Of course, *every* conclusion should restate the thesis—you have one final shot at driving home the point of the entire sermon. But in a deductive pattern you have been stating your thesis in one form or another repeatedly throughout the entire sermon—proving it, explaining it, applying it, unpacking it. Since the inductive sermon holds the answer until the end, you need to give it some extra attention. Illustrate it if it will help. Give a real-life example your audience can latch onto. Perhaps find the big idea as worded by another preacher or scholar in case your wording doesn't cut it for them. Keep it varied, but do whatever you have to in order to ensure that if your listeners are interviewed after the service, they can nail your basic thesis, in their words or yours.

Some sermons will bring home the application toward the end. Others will have application interspersed throughout. In either case, the conclusion is not the place to store your application material. The conclusion should not contain new information. It should be the last attempt, in about a paragraph or two, to ensure that the overarching question has been answered. The reason I say that the primary purpose of the conclusion is to answer the overarching question is because that is the primary purpose of teaching God's word in any context. Sure we must apply it. But if I don't understand what I'm applying, I can't do it. Application may have been offered at different points along the way in the sermon. Application may have been saved for the end, just before the conclusion. But the primary function of the conclusion is to make sure that what was promised in the introduction is clearly delivered—to remind them of the truth that they are applying.

Nor is the conclusion the place to simply restate everything that was just preached but in a shorter form. It is harder to sound more boring than to, in effect, say something like, "Okay, let's start back up at the top but quickly this time. Remember, point one was ..." Besides killing listener interest, this type of conclusion does not do its job. The job is not to cover every place we have been. It is to clarify our destination. Restating is more than repeating—it's a gestalt. It's the light bulb coming on for your listeners as they see all the explanations, proofs, illustrations, and applications come together, bringing home one solid idea that they can take with them.

CONCLUSION

The effective introduction introduces the need for the text, and the effective conclusion serves to ensure the resolution is absolutely clear. Keep the approach varied, but not gimmicky. Use whatever rhetorical device is at your disposal to raise the overarching question or to make the answer as unambiguous as possible, but make sure you use it for clarity. Don't labor for hours over what fresh story or movie reference you might use. And don't insert one because "that's what intros and conclusions do." A succinct paragraph with no anecdote or special quote is just fine so long as the thesis statement is unmistakably explicit. Begin with a compelling invitation to discover your listeners' need for the text, and leave them with no doubt as to what the text has resolved for them.

Conclusion

I knew exactly what the preacher was going to say next. I leaned over to my wife and told her what his next point would be. Within seconds the preacher fulfilled my prophecy. Next, I leaned over and told her what illustration would follow. I nailed it again.

Now, my wife knows I am no seer. She must have thought the preacher, someone I knew, shared his notes with me beforehand. He didn't. But I did see his notes, in a sense. I had been browsing sermon manuscripts online the night before to see how other preachers handled a text that I was studying at the time. I came across an interesting sermon that happened to be on a different passage. As I listened to the preacher, it took me a few minutes to figure out why I felt I had heard it before. I hadn't. I'd read it before.

This preacher had given no credit to his online source. Since I knew him personally, I decided to quietly and carefully confront him for plagiarism in the pulpit. Naturally, he was embarrassed. *Super*naturally, he received the rebuke with humility. When he explained why he did it, I felt a kind of solidarity with him: it was the pressure of preparation. Each week rushes in with a deluge of assignments and meetings, emails and appointments. He felt suffocated by the overwhelming tasks, and he reached for a lifeline late Saturday night. I knew he would never do it again. Better to preach a poor sermon than to be dishonest with your congregation.

But will it suffice to preach a poor sermon? I know I have preached many a sermon that could have been better had I put more effort into it. Had I not waited so long to begin my preparation. Had I not allowed myself to get so busy with other things. Am I a better man for preaching a poor sermon when I could have been clearer, smoother, more in tune with the text, better poised to explain it well? You can catch plagiarism. It's hard to catch lack of diligence. May the Lord grant us the humility I saw in my pastor friend that day so that we can also accept the rebuke: preaching takes work and we need to get to it for every sermon.

This book was not designed to increase your workload but to relieve it. The purpose is to increase your effectiveness while streamlining your sermon work. You can preach an engaging, attention-commanding sermon *with* your exposition of the text. You don't need to exegete the text and then spend an equal amount of time searching for amusing stories or entertaining visuals as you do studying the biblical text.

If you spend long hours preparing slides with images and attractive backgrounds, securing exotic props like zoo animals or ancient relics, or working through stacks of magazines and newspapers just to illustrate a point, you are misunderstanding preaching. Especially if it compromises time needed to gain a thorough grasp of the text. You are misguided if you think that in order to be engaging you must interpolate attention-grabbing devices throughout the sermon. As I have said throughout, this is not to say that relevant anecdotes or analogies are bad. They're great! But being a slave to them is bad. Crowding your already congested schedule with hours of labor over how to keep your listeners interested is working against you. The old adage is true: work smarter, not harder.

The smart way is to engage your listeners with tension that is continuous and lasting rather than sporadic. You capture their interest with the reason this Scripture passage exists—the need it exposes—and hold their attention with it throughout the sermon. This puts the spotlight on the exposition and keeps it there. This is smart work that creates less work, for the listener and for you.

After reading this book and being confronted with a new way of thinking about sermon preparation, you might feel overwhelmed. Perhaps you've been preaching in a certain way for so long that changing now feels like an immense task. Whittling your sermon down to one thesis statement instead of several equal points might be new to you. Thinking in terms of sermon patterns or introducing an overarching question into the equation may seem like you're adding work. But it's subtraction by addition.

I used to help my uncle when he owned a landscaping company. When we wrapped up each job, I would strap on the leaf blower and make sure the streets and walking paths were clear of debris. My uncle would get irritated when I took longer than he wanted, but what could I do? That was just how long it took, right? My problem was that I double-backed. A lot. I took longer than I should have because I was working against myself. My uncle knew a way to do the same work in a much more efficient way. He had a pattern, and eventually I learned that pattern. Going from having a poor plan to adopting someone else's strategy seemed hard at first. There was a hump of rethinking, pride swallowing, and frustration that I had to get over. But when I did, our jobs were finished a lot sooner.

If much of what you have read here is new to you but you see value in the approach, don't let the difficulty of relearning intimidate you. At first it will take you longer to craft your message around one problem-solution than it currently takes you to prepare a multiple-point sermon. But soon you will wonder how you found the time to develop several ideas instead of one! At first you will feel the frustration of trying one sermon structure, only to figure out later that another would have been more effective. But one day you might come across an old sermon outline and wonder how you didn't confuse yourself, let alone your congregation.

You can overcome the temptation to retreat to your old ways by committing to take one step at a time. Take one principle from this book and do not dwell on the rest until you have demonstrated a level of proficiency there. Go in order. If you are not preaching expository messages, fix that first—ignore the rest of this book until then. Once you are consistent in sound exposition you can move on to structuring your sermon to maintain tension. Start with articulating the thesis of the passage. Craft a sermon that drives home that one thesis the entire way. When you hit a stride, take on the challenges of choosing structures that fit, introductions that grab attention, and pointing listeners to the ultimate solution in Christ.

Over time you will master the components in this book and then some. There is more to commanding attention than any one book can cover. You can develop your storytelling skills. You will notice that when you are touching directly on a topic that is burning in everyone's minds at the moment, attention is given freely. You can make effective use of pitch, pace, tone, inflection. You can learn about the use of your facial expressions and body language. You can study proxemics and how your physical distance in relation to your listeners has an effect on your

communication. But to begin, focus on one thing at a t...
with the suggestions here and commit to making progress.

With each step you will notice improvement, and so will your regular listeners. Take joy in the improvements, and do not allow the long road ahead to discourage you. It is not as long as it might seem. It's like physical training. With each workout you can accomplish more than you could when you first started. As you master each principle laid out in this book, the next will be adopted more easily, learned more quickly. I am still learning with every sermon I preach.

But ultimately, this is not a strategy to prepare your sermons faster. In the long-run, I do believe this is a more efficient approach to sermon preparation, but only as a perk, an added benefit. It will help with the pressure of Sunday's looming deadline, but mainly this approach is about wielding your exposition to preach sermons that engage the listener well. You are not diluting or stepping away from exposition to command attention; you are commanding attention with your exposition. You demonstrate to the audience that the text in front of them exposes a real need. Then you show them how the text provides the solution or the answer. This is preaching with tension. Not as a mere rhetorical strategy, but in the understanding that this is how Scripture functions.

Preach to give your listeners truth they cannot ignore. Preach to fill up what is lacking in their faith and point them to Christ. Preach to capture and keep their voluntary interest. This is preaching that is worthy of being heard.

EXERCISE 1

Practice Determining Thesis Statements

Examine the following texts selected from various sources, beginning with nonbiblical literature and moving into examples from Scripture. Articulate the thesis (a subject and a complement, or a question and answer) for each citation. Remember, you are not looking for the only way it can possibly be worded, but keep working at it until you think you have found a statement that best represents the subject and complement of the text. Then compare your results with those provided at the end of this section.

EXAMPLE

"Throughout our discussion of prayer in the Psalms, we have found prayer to be the believer's source of courage and strength, and the Israelite's weapon against the enemy. The book of Psalms is far more than a mere collection of prayers. It powerfully teaches us to seek the Lord in all our varied human conditions.

That was the means by which the psalmist experienced peace in this life."[101]

First, what is the paragraph saying?

> Subject: The book of Psalms teaches us to pray ... (or) *Why* does the book of Psalms teach us to pray?

Second, what is it saying about that subject? How does it answer the question?

> Complement: ... in order that we might experience peace in the Lord.

Discovering the complement helps you to see that the proper question is "why" in this case, and not "how" or "when," for example.

EXERCISES

1. "**Irregardless**. Should be *regardless*. The error results from failure to see the negative in *-less* and from a desire to get it in as a prefix, suggested by such words as *irregular, irresponsible,* and, perhaps especially, *irrespective*."[102]

   Subject: ____

   ____

   Complement: ____

   ____

---

101. Kyu Nam Jung, "Prayer in the Psalms," in *Teach Us to Pray: Prayer in the Bible and the World*, ed. D. A. Carson (Eugene, OR: Wipf and Stock, 2002), 57.

102. William Strunk Jr. and E. B. White, *The Elements of Style*, 4th ed. (New York: Longman Publishers, 2000), 50.

2. "It was Smoke's varied play that obfuscated them. Sometimes, consulting his notebook or engaging in long calculations, an hour elapsed without his staking a chip. At other times, he would win three limit-bets and clean up a thousand dollars and odd, in five or ten minutes. At still other times, his tactics would be to scatter single chips prodigally and amazingly over the table. This would continue for from ten to thirty minutes of play, when, abruptly, as the ball whirled through the last of its circles, he would play the limit on column, color, and number, and win all three. Once, to complete confusion in the minds of those that strove to divine his secret, he lost forty straight bets, each at the limit. But each night, play no matter how diversely, Shorty carried home thirty-five hundred dollars for him."[103]

   Subject: ______________________________

   ____

   Complement: ______________________________

   ____

3. "And before we judge of (the Martians) too harshly we must remember what ruthless and utter destruction our own species has wrought, not only upon animals, such as the vanished bison and the dodo, but upon its own inferior races. The Tasmanians, in spite of their human likeness, were entirely swept out of existence in a war of extermination waged by European immigrants, in the space of fifty years. Are we such apostles of mercy as to complain if the Martians warred in the same spirit?"[104]

103. Jack London, *Smoke Bellew* (Mineola, NY: 1992), 60.
104. H. G. Wells, *The War of the Worlds* (New York: Scholastic, 2005), 10.

Subject: ______________________________

____

Complement: ______________________________

____

4. "Many things said about God in previous chapters could also be said of the God of other religions, especially monotheistic ones, such as Judaism and Islam. The doctrine of the Trinity, however, is a uniquely Christian doctrine. Some may think this doctrine is not so special after all, for many religions worship multiple gods, and this doctrine makes Christianity a form of polytheism. However, that clearly misunderstands what Christians mean in asserting that God is triune. Christianity insists that only one God exists, but it is just as emphatic in maintaining that the Father, the Son, and the Holy Spirit all are God."[105]

Subject: ______________________________

____

Complement: ______________________________

____

5. "In exposition of Old Testament narratives, it's better to concentrate on preaching scene by scene or paragraph by paragraph than verse by verse. Take Genesis 38 as an example. While preachers will work through the entire narrative, they may quickly summarize the events in verses 1–11 without pausing for extended analysis."[106]

---

105. John S. Feinberg, *No One Like Him* (Wheaton, IL: Crossway, 2001), 437.

106. Steven D. Mathewson, *The Art of Preaching Old Testament Narrative* (Grand Rapids: Baker Academic, 2002), 22.

Subject: ____

____

Complement:_____________________________________

____

6. "Praise the Lord, all nations! Extol him, all peoples! For great is his steadfast love toward us, and the faithfulness of the Lord endures forever. Praise the Lord!" (Ps 117:1–2)

   Subject: ____

   ____

   Complement:_____________________________________

   ____

7. "But we do not want you to be uninformed, brothers, about those who are asleep, that you may not grieve as others do who have no hope. For since we believe that Jesus died and rose again, even so, through Jesus, God will bring with him those who have fallen asleep. For this we declare to you by a word from the Lord, that we who are alive, who are left until the coming of the Lord, will not precede those who have fallen asleep. For the Lord himself will descend from heaven with a cry of command, with the voice of an archangel, and with the sound of the trumpet of God. And the dead in Christ will rise first. Then we who are alive, who are left, will be caught up together with them in the clouds to meet the Lord in the air, and so we will always be with the Lord. Therefore encourage one another with these words." (1 Thess 4:13–18)

   Subject: ____

   ____

Complement: ______________________________________

____

8. "Beloved, I urge you as sojourners and exiles to abstain from the passions of the flesh, which wage war against your soul. Keep your conduct among the Gentiles honorable, so that when they speak against you as evildoers, they may see your good deeds and glorify God on the day of visitation." (1 Pet 2:11–12)

   Subject: ______________________________________

   ____

   Complement: ___________________________________

   ____

9. "My son, if you receive my words and treasure up my commandments with you, making your ear attentive to wisdom and inclining you heart to understanding; yes, if you call out for insight and raise your voice for understanding, if you seek it like silver and search for it as hidden treasures, then you will understand the fear of the LORD and find the knowledge of God." (Prov 2:1–5)

   Subject: ______________________________________

   ____

   Complement: ___________________________________

   ____

10. "This is why I left you in Crete, so that you might put what remained into order, and appoint elders in every town as I directed you—if anyone is above reproach, the husband of one wife, and his children are believers and not open to

the charge of debauchery or insubordination. For an overseer, as God's steward, must be above reproach. He must not be arrogant or quick-tempered or a drunkard or violent or greedy for gain, but hospitable, a lover of good, self-controlled, upright, holy, and disciplined. He must hold firm to the trustworthy word as taught, so that he may be able to give instruction in sound doctrine and also to rebuke those who contradict it." (Titus 1:5–9)

Subject: ______________________________

____

Complement: ______________________________

____

SUGGESTED ANSWERS

These are not meant to serve as infallible answers. Yours may differ slightly. You will likely be able to improve on these and get closer to that ideal center of the target. If you think an answer here is better than the one you wrote, do not be discouraged! This discipline takes time to develop; but rest assured, with practice you will get it.

Also, you may have some of these in the reverse order to the answers provided. You might have made the subject the complement and the complement the subject. Try to look at the text and ask yourself how the author is going about it. Normally, you will be able to see that if the subject and the complement are reversed, the thesis either becomes untrue or does not quite match the agenda of the text.

1. **Subject:** The word "irregardless" should not be used. (Why?)
   Complement: Because it contains a double negative.

2. **Subject**: Smoke's winning strategy was difficult for others to figure out. (Why?)
   Complement: Because he varied his play.
3. **Subject**: We have no place to complain about merciless invaders. (Why?)
   Complement: Because we are guilty of the same ruthlessness.
4. **Subject**: The doctrine of the Trinity is uniquely Christian. (How?)
   Complement: It affirms the existence of one God while also emphasizing this God is triune.
5. **Subject**: A preacher should move the listener through Old Testament narrative. (How?)
   Complement: Scene by scene rather than line by line.
6. **Subject**: All people should praise the Lord. (Why?)
   Complement: Because of his unwavering love toward us.
7. **Subject**: We must understand the resurrection of the saints. (Why?)
   Complement: In order to grieve loss with hope.
8. **Subject**: We must live honorable lives among unbelievers. (Why?)
   Complement: So that by witnessing our behavior, they might ultimately be saved.
9. **Subject**: We can come to know God. (When?)
   Complement: When we diligently seek his wisdom.
10. **Subject**: Elders must be appointed who are above reproach. (Why?)
    Complement: Because they must live the truths they are entrusted to protect.

EXERCISE 2

Practice Choosing Sermon Structures

Examine the following passages of Scripture. Think about which sermon pattern might be a good fit with the way the passage unfolds and write down your choice below each passage. Choose between the four patterns discussed in chapter 3: inductive, deductive, inductive-deductive, and subject-completed. Compare your answers with those provided at the end of this section, but keep in mind that there is flexibility here. Your answers may differ but that doesn't mean they are "wrong." Many passages will work with more than one pattern. Choose which you think is best considering what you have learned in this book.

EXERCISES

1. Read: Romans 13:1–7

   Structure: ______________________________

2. Read: Psalm 1

   Structure: ______________________________

3. Read: Psalm 119:9–16

   Structure: ________________________________

4. Read: Luke 9:46–48

   Structure: ________________________________

5. Read: Hebrews 13:17

   Structure: ________________________________

SUGGESTED ANSWERS

1. Read: Romans 13:1–7
   Structure: *Deductive*

   Paul begins with the subject (we must submit to the governing authorities) and immediately provides the complement (because their authority is from God). What follows is not a list of other complements, but rather explanations of the one complement provided at the outset. Those governing authorities are instituted by God (end of v. 1), appointed by God (v. 2). They are servants of God (twice in v. 4) and they carry out God's wrath (v. 4). They are to be feared because they are ministers of God (v. 6). It is not that there is no new information past verse 1; it is that everything past verse 1 explains or applies verse 1. We must obey governing authorities because their authority is from God.

2. Read: Psalm 1
   Structure: *Inductive-Deductive*

   The psalm is answering the question: "Who is the blessed man?" But the answer is not given immediately. First, we are told what a blessed person is *not*. Nor is the answer given at the end of the psalm—it's given in verse 2 (it is the person who delights in God's Law). Since the preacher will probably take time to unpack the rest of verse 1 (what the blessed person is *not*), the listener is not getting the answer right away. Therefore, a deductive pattern is probably less helpful. But a fully inductive sermon will not work either since the answer arrives in verse 2. An inductive-deductive sermon would work well here. Remember, for an inductive-deductive sermon, the thesis does not have to appear in the exact middle of the sermon's body or the exact middle of the text. It's just that the complement is not given in the introduction and it is not given at the end of the body. It can appear *anywhere* between the introduction and the end of the sermon's body.

3. Read: Psalm 119:9–16
   Structure: *Deductive*

   This passage does begin with a question and it is not rhetorical. It begs for an answer. But it does not work well with an inductive sermon pattern because the answer is provided too soon. The second line in verse 9 provides the complement. The other seven verses in this passage unpack what is meant by that answer.

4. Read: Luke 9:46–48
   Structure: *Inductive*

   The paragraph essentially begins with an argument over a question as to what greatness is. The disciples' specific question was regarding which one of them was the greatest. But Jesus knew the "reasoning of their hearts" and exposed that they really did not understand greatness. Therefore, the question the passage really is setting out to answer is, "What is real greatness?" There's the subject. The passage does not give a full answer right away. Curiosity is provoked as Jesus brings a child to his side. Jesus offers a somewhat cryptic explanation in the beginning of verse 48, but then makes it clear in the last line: "For he who is least among you all is the one who is great." There is the complement.

5. Read: Hebrews 13:17
   Structure: *Subject-Completed*

   The subject is that we should obey our leaders. Then two complements are provided in the rest of the verse. The first is a reason *why* we should obey our leaders (they have to give an account), and the second is a statement about *how* we should obey our leaders (to let them watch over us with joy). I might try to use one complement that covers both the *why* and the *how*—but when it starts feeling forced, I might concede that the text really does provide two complements here. In that case, I would use the subject-completed pattern.

APPENDIX A

Resolving to Preach Expositionally

Preaching must be expository ...

Otherwise there is no authority in what is preached.

The Bible is authoritative because it is God's word. If I am not saying what it is saying, then I am not speaking with divine authority. If I am not speaking with authority, then why should anyone listen to what I have to say?

So that I will not infringe upon Christ's headship of the church.

If I am taking authority into my own hands, then I am in effect usurping Christ's role as head of the church. But since I am not the head of the church, then I must stick to Christ's marching orders as revealed in all of Scripture and make them plain to the congregation.

So that I know I am ministering in concert with the Holy Spirit.

Many preachers pray that God would fill them with the Spirit in their preaching, and rightly so. Some would say they need not prepare because they will simply depend on the Spirit's guidance in what they say, and wrongly so. We must consider that since the Holy Spirit produced Scripture (inspiration) and is the One who helps us truly grasp it (illumination), then we must preach what Scripture says if we are to minister in step with the Spirit. I step away from the ministry of the Holy Spirit when I step away from the intended import of his text.

For the preaching to be truly transformative.

Scripture is inspired to be written just the way it is for the purpose of equipping the believer with what is needed to be complete and ready for every good work (2 Tim 3:16–17). Preaching is how a pastor equips, reproves, rebukes, and exhorts his congregation (2 Tim 3:16–4:2). Without preaching that carefully expounds the words of Scripture, the people are left ill-equipped for change and growth.

To join the Lord in exalting his name and his word above all things (Ps 138:2).

Clearly, if I am not sticking to what the word of God says, then I am not rejoicing in it the way God is. Instead, I am only rejoicing in what I can do with it.

So that people learn how to read the Bible for themselves.

How can they learn what the Bible says if I am not showing them what it actually says? If I insert my own thoughts according to some arbitrary hermeneutic, how can the people follow my logic? They will go home more dependent on the preacher who has special interpretations and less dependent on Scripture.

To draw appropriate connections between interpretation and application.

This is perhaps what most Bible readers have the most difficult time understanding. We need to show them how to apply the word responsibly or no one else will. We must first understand the meaning of a text before we can understand how it is significant to us today.

To protect the church from false teaching (Titus 1:9).

If I make a claim on my own authority when I preach and someone else makes a contradictory claim on their own authority in my church, how can this be resolved? We must stand on the authority of Scripture as the standard against which all truth claims are measured.

To better understand what we are proclaiming when we sing songs laden with scriptural allusions, quotes, and references.

When a church uses songs with lyrics paraphrasing or quoting Scripture, how can the people understand what they are singing if we are not explaining those texts to them? We cannot worship in truth if we do not understand what that truth is.

To bolster their reason to praise the Lord (Ps 119:62).

"At midnight I rise to praise you because of your righteous rules." What God says inspires what his people sing. If I am preaching something else, then I am robbing them of this inspiration or giving them false inspiration, no matter how moving I perceive my words to be.

To build our trust in God's promises.

If we tell people something is true when it is not what God's word says, they will eventually realize it is not true. But they will think it is God's word that is not true because they learned the lie from a sermon. If we only preach truth, then they will see that God's word never fails. And in order for them to make that connection, we need to be able to show them how we got that truth from *this* text.

So the people will know the Lord's will (Ps 40:8).

"I delight to do your will O my God, your law is within my heart." The reason why the psalmist delights to do God's will is because Scripture is in his heart. He understands what it is calling him to do. Our people will not be able to know what God really expects of them if we are not accurately teaching them what Scripture says.

To feed souls that are consumed with longing for God's word (Ps 119:20).

"My soul is consumed with longing for your rules at all times." If I am not giving them God's rules and essentially making up my own rules instead, then I cannot feed souls that are hungry for only what God actually says.

To build the hearers' trust in the preacher.

If I am saying, "This is what God's word says" and it really isn't, then over time people will discover that I am not to be trusted. I am not speaking truth. Even if I am speaking the right truth from the wrong place—a *common* infraction—I am still not being truthful because I am purporting, "This text says this," when it doesn't.

To ensure my favorite subjects don't dominate the pulpit.

If I am committed to preaching what the Bible says, then I will more likely stretch out past my comfort zone when it comes to the subjects of my sermons. I will allow the passage, whatever it says, to inform what I say. This is why it is a good idea to preach through books of the Bible instead of a different verse from a different book every Sunday—we're allowing the book of the Bible, passage by passage, to control our direction. This discipline also helps guard against the misuse of the pulpit to advance personal agendas. If I am constrained by what the Bible says, then I will not allow issues to take over that have nothing to do with the text in front of me.[107]

So when I am confronted about something I said, I can point to Scripture.

When I am questioned about something I said in a sermon, I am not offended and I don't take it personally. When someone challenges me concerning something I said, I am obligated to justify it. But if I am preaching God's word, all I have to do is show how this is what *God says.* They are taking issue with the text, not with me.[108]

Many more can be added but it should be clear that this is not simply about preaching style. It is not that expository preaching is for the studious, bookworm types and some other kind of preaching is for the more relational, visionary types. Expository preaching is the pastor's *job,* and without it, the church cannot be shepherded effectively. It is the preacher committed to faithfully communicating the meaning of a particular portion

---

107. There is a place for topical sermons. Issues come up that may need to be addressed from the pulpit, and the preacher may need to use various passages or perhaps one passage detached from a series in that biblical book. This can still be done in an expository way, but the preacher will find it wise to not make this the regular weekly pattern.

108. Of course, there are those times where my interpretation of the text is what is being questioned, but no one can accuse me of hijacking or ignoring the text if I can demonstrate how I came to my conclusion from what Scripture says.

of Scripture who is able to preach with authority and humility. It is the expository preacher delivering Spirit-empowered sermons who sees true transformation in people. Exposition teaches a congregation to exalt God's word, to read it, to interpret, and apply it rightly, and to use it to discern false teaching. It is vital for church health because it informs and inspires our singing. It builds our trust in God's promises and teaches us his will. It is the only way to really feed hungry souls. Expository preaching protects preachers from accusation and from their own misguided proclivities. And without expository preaching, a dangerous attrition of trust between congregation and preacher is inevitable. Whatever your background, whatever your personality, if you are a preacher, you must commit to clear and careful exposition.

EXPOSITORY PREACHING SELF-EXAM

I have come across preachers who believe they are faithfully expositional but whose sermons prove otherwise. They probably think, "Well, my sermons have Bible verses in them, don't they?" Not all who describe themselves as expository preachers really are. Self-awareness does not always come easy, but there are symptoms that can alert the preacher to the disease. Others of us are on a path of growth. My sermons are more expositional now than they were when I first committed to exposition. Every once in a while, we should reflect on our preaching and test it for adherence to exposition.

Take a moment to give your preaching a brief health checkup. The following set of questions can serve as a basic diagnostic tool in this regard. They are not exhaustive, but they should begin to either admonish or affirm your philosophy of preaching. After praying that God would grant you the grace to be thoroughly honest with yourself, walk through this list of twelve questions, answering either "Yes" or "No" along the way:

1. If you swapped your Scripture passage with another, would the rest of the sermon stay pretty much the same?

2. Do you consistently use several passages to compose a sermon rather than staying in one paragraph or story?

3. Do you typically begin your sermon preparation by looking for a passage to explain your point rather than looking *into* a passage to *discover* its point?

4. Do you spend equal or more time researching illustrations, anecdotes, analogies, and props than you do the passage itself?

5. Do you tend to present the passage as a list of points that really don't exist as stand-alone points in the passage?

6. Do people generally give you feedback that they are impressed at your ability to find meaning in ways they would never be able to?

7. Do people generally give you feedback that they understand the passage better as a result of your sermon?

8. Do you take the time to discover why the author placed this paragraph here and not in some other place in the book?

9. Do you consider what we would be missing if this passage were never written?

10. Do you feel like you trust in the raw power of your Scripture passage more than in your power to deliver it?

11. Do you find the plain truths of the Bible engaging enough to not have to reach for something new to say?

12. Have you sometimes had to change your direction (sermon title, theme for the worship service, how the sermon fits into a series) because your study of the passage has altered your previous understanding of it?

The first six questions serve as checks to warn us—each one serves as a sort of "check engine" light to prompt your pulling over to address some things. If your answer to all or most of the first six questions is "Yes," then you may want to rethink how you prepare sermons because they are probably not faithful to the text of Scripture on a consistent basis. Even if you still preach truth, if it is not truth derived from the text in front of you, then you are operating outside the bounds of your role as a preacher. You are there to teach what the word of God says and to show them from Scripture how this is what it says. Your passage should direct your entire sermon, not just be incidental to it (question #1). You should feel that most of the time everything you need to communicate a powerful, truth-packed, relevant, life-changing sermon is contained in one passage of Scripture.[109]

---

109. There are times when multiple verses from varying passages may be quite appropriate. With "doctrinal preaching," for example, you are building a case for a confessional stance on a topic and perhaps no one verse gives the full

You shouldn't feel compelled to stack various verses together to preach a sermon (question #2). At least half of your time, if not more, should be spent laboring in the passage seeking to find what the text truly communicates. The sermon process is not an idea looking for a home in Scripture. It's Scripture giving you the idea that you will preach (question #3). This means that if your sermon prep time gets cut short somehow, the delivery side of your preaching suffers, not the content of your preaching (question #4). Your content is controlled by the text; the text is not controlled by your content (question #5). Finally (question #6), your goal in preaching is for your feedback to sound like, "Wow, pastor, thank you. I really understand that passage now!" You might be in trouble if your feedback consistently sounds like, "Wow, pastor, I have no idea how you got that from this passage—you must really have an interpretive gift!"

Conversely, the second half of the diagnostic questions above serves to affirm your preaching if you are faithful to the text in your sermons. If you answered "Yes" to the last six questions, you are probably right on track with the true task of preaching. We want our listeners to understand the passage, not just our sermon (question #7). We want to allow the immediate context of the current passage to inform the direction of the sermon. Not only do we not take verses out of context, but we don't take paragraphs, chapters, or whole books out of context either (question #8). At the same time, we want to point out the particular and unique point of revelation that each passage offers (question #9).[110] We trust that this passage was inspired for a reason

picture of that particular doctrine. One might also have a small text, such as a proverb, in which case the preacher might find it wise to show how this text is explained or applied by other texts of Scripture.

110. This is not to say that each section of Scripture contains truth that can be found nowhere else. It is to say that each passage is profitable in its own way.

and that it is profitable without my help (question #10). We don't need to embellish it or improve upon it in any way (question #11). And because Scripture has the first and last say, we will bend over backward to make sure everything else falls in line with it, even when it is inconvenient (question #12).

We should consider how *this* passage conveys this truth in ways that others do not. What does this passage add to what we know from other places in Scripture? In short, what would we be missing if this passage did not exist? Why did God inspire *this* portion of Scripture?

APPENDIX B

Sample Map of a Sermon Series on Exodus

The following is a map of a sermon series I gave on the book of Exodus. I have included my thesis statement for each, as well as the structure and the overarching question(s). I have also included at the end of each unit my reasoning for why I divided the pericopes where I did. Introductions, segues, and conclusions are not included—the purpose here is for you to see the strategy in dividing preaching units. Where the connection to Christ is evident in the text, the thesis statement will reflect the ultimate solution. Where the ultimate solution is not as clear from the passage, it will be made clear in the sermon, but the thesis statement will not reflect it.

You can use these to help you think through the principles explained in this book. Your decisions may look different, and I trust that you can improve on this map. My hope is that it will serve you and, through you, your highly engaged listeners!

THESIS OF THE BOOK OF EXODUS

The book of Exodus demonstrates that God delivers his people from a bondage to slavery that they could not cast off themselves.

Secondary themes include the fact that God delivers in such a way as to make it known that his intervention is the only possible explanation, that God orchestrates time, events, and people in order to accomplish his rescue, and that God's rescue is a process requiring faith but moving from bondage to exit to journey to conquer and rest.

EXODUS 3:15; 12:1–3, 5, 10, 17; 15:12–14

Thesis Statement (TS): We interpret the book of Exodus rightly when we understand it serves as a picture of the gospel.

Structure: *Deductive*. I am setting out to prove my thesis, which will be new to some, possibly objectionable to others.

Overarching Question (OQ): We often read the Bible as a "how-to" book, but that's not right; so how should I approach reading a book like Exodus rightly? Is it *really* about the gospel?

Reasoning: This is the first time I have introduced a book by not beginning with the first pericope. But since many downplay the gospel in Exodus or do not see it there at all, I wanted to provide the rationale behind preaching the gospel in Exodus before diving in. I drew parallels between the Israelite experience in Exodus and our own pilgrimage in Christ. I also drew parallels between Israel and Jesus, who fulfills the role on our behalf that neither Israel nor we could fulfill. The primary application to draw is that God rescues sinners from bondage to sin and death. The starting point was Genesis 3:15.

EXODUS 1:1–2:10

TS: We should fear God more than man because God always gets his way.

Structure: *Inductive*. The complement that God always gets his way is expressed climactically in the final move of the passage (2:1–10), and I also elaborate specifically on 1:12, 17, and 21 in this final portion of the sermon.

OQ: Why don't we fear God? Or, better, what is it that we really need to understand about God in order to fear him as we should?

Reasoning: I marked this as a unit because I saw fear as a unifying theme. Pharaoh and his oppression certainly induced the temptation to fear that God had abandoned his promise to deliver his people. Pharaoh feared. He feared that the Hebrews would prove too mighty to deal with if they choose to unite with an enemy of Egypt (1:9–10, 12). The midwives feared. They disobeyed Pharaoh's order because they feared God more than they feared Egypt (1:17, 21). Ultimately God is the one to be feared because he is the one who gets his way no matter the opposition (1:12, 17, 21; 2:1–10).

EXODUS 2:11–3:22

TS: We are not ready to be delivered by God from bondage until we reckon with our complete inability to rescue ourselves.

Structure: *Inductive*. I begin by explaining that we see in Moses what we often see in ourselves—a desire to self-motivate, to be our own source of rescue. The final portion of the pericope (3:13–22) climaxes with the clear complement.

OQ: Especially in light of the problem of false conversions in the church, how do we know we are at the point where we *really* understand God's plan of deliverance?

Reasoning: In this unit, Moses seeks to take things into his own hands by jump-starting his role as deliverer (Acts 7:25). It backfires, and he ends up in a place where he recognizes he is nothing but an alien in a strange land (Exod 2:22). Here, God teaches him that his role as deliverer has nothing to do with his qualifications. Rather, it has everything to do with God's qualifications. Moses asks, "Who am I to deliver?" and this is exactly where Moses needs to be. God answers by explaining that deliverance from bondage is about "Who *I* AM." I cut it off mid-conversation not only because it would otherwise make for a very long preaching unit, but because in chapter 3, the focus is God establishing his own centrality to the rescue of the Israelites. Chapter 4 highlights Moses' response of obedience in faith (trust in God's sovereignty over the mouth, trust that the signs will work, that the serpent will not bite him, that Aaron will help, and so forth).

EXODUS 4:1–17

TS: We will grow in obedience to God when we learn to trust him by faith.

Structure: *Deductive*. Right away the passage gets into God meeting Moses' need by helping his unbelief, which points us to the complement. Rather than leaving them wondering what this conversation has to do with the subject, I am giving them the complement up front and then using the conversation to explain the complement.

OQ: Does God ask us to trust him blindly? Does he understand how difficult it is to follow him when we can't see ahead?

Reasoning: I was going to preach through to the end of chapter 4, but the episode in verses 24–26 prompted me to change my mind for two reasons: A) I thought that verses 1–17 focused on the command for Moses to go and the dynamics of faith and disbelief at work in Moses. The rest of the chapter is about his going and the strange episode with the circumcision, which I take to be about Moses' readiness to go. That is, he cannot bring a word/message of deliverance to his people if he and his household are not fully protected by the covenant. B) Since the circumcision episode is difficult to understand and widely debated, I wanted to slow down and unpack what's happening there. That might be too long of an excursus in another sermon, so I wrote it as its own sermon.

EXODUS 4:18–31

TS: We cannot be a part of God's program for rescue if we are not ourselves covered by His covenant with us.

Structure: *Inductive-Deductive*. The sermon will begin by looking at differing interpretations, casting doubt on them in light of the text. Then what I understand to be the most reasonable interpretation is presented around the middle of the sermon. I then proceed to defend it from the text.

OQ a: How are we to understand these two cryptic verses that seem really confusing? **OQ b:** Why is that the right interpretation? *Remember: Sometimes the point of tension for entrance into the sermon can be simply the difficulty of understanding the text.*

Reasoning: Since this portion is difficult to understand, I thought I should give it the full attention of one whole sermon. At any rate, if my interpretation is correct (see the above thesis statement), its purpose is different enough from 4:1–17 for it to demand its own sermon.

EXODUS 4:21; 5:1–23; 6:1; 7:3

TS: God may embolden his opposition in order to demonstrate his absolute sovereignty in victory.

Structure: *Inductive-Deductive*. For this one, I spend some time pointing out the verses that raise this difficult concept (God's hardening of Pharaoh's heart) and I let them "bother" us for a little bit. Then partway through I provide the answer, which is not immediately satisfying. But I set out to explain it from Scripture in the second portion of the sermon.

OQ a: Why would God harden a man's heart? That's not fair is it? That's not free will! **OQ b**: Is that really the reason? I was taught differently—is this clear in the text?

Reasoning: The hardening of Pharaoh's heart is mentioned in several places. I wanted to take one sermon to address the "elephant in the room" and treat the difficulty many have with the fact that God sovereignly hardened a heart such that the person would not be able to obey the commands issued by God. Thus, instead of staying in one thought unit, for this sermon I took the relevant verses in Exodus and put them together for a sort of "theology of hardening." The texts listed above served the primary role, but other verses in Exodus were listed and briefly referred to in the sermon as well. In the second half of the sermon, I incorporated New Testament passages as well to make sure the listeners understood that the Bible is consistent on this matter.

EXODUS 7–10

TS: God's fierce demonstrations of power are to help us teach our children that God alone is deserving of worship.

Structure: *Inductive*. The fierceness and strangeness of the plagues sustains the tension of the OQ until the answer is finally revealed in 10:1–2.

OQ: Why did God bring about such horrible plagues on people in Exodus? Is this what the New Testament God is like? Why such fierce measures?

Reasoning: Of course, I did not read and explain every verse and every line in these four chapters. I read verses 7:1–13 straight through as a setup for explaining the plagues that follow, which are a preview of what is going to transpire across the upcoming plagues. Then I summarized and explained each plague. I covered the first nine plagues because they appear to form three sets of three plagues each. Rather than preaching one sermon per plague or one per set, I decided to preach all nine together. The primary idea of each set is the same and the rhetorical effect of their rapid succession is preserved when preaching them together. The sermon culminated in a focus on verses 10:1–2 demonstrating that the purpose of the plagues was to provide Israel with content by which they would catechize their children. The point of the lesson is that Yahweh is an idol-crushing God; there is none like him.

EXODUS 11:1–13:16

TS: We must always remember the tenth plague because, through the celebration of the Lord's Supper, we remember we are "passed over" only in Jesus Christ.

Structure: *Inductive-Deductive*. The sermon will begin by exploring this final plague—how absolutely tragic it was but also how emphatic the Lord was about remembering it. This presses the tension of the OQ for the inductive portion. At some point, I reveal the complement and then draw the connections for them the rest of the way.

OQ a: Why is the most devastating plague the basis of a tradition that was to be strictly remembered? **OQ b:** How are the Passover and the Lord's Supper connected? How does the former help deepen our understanding of the latter?

Reasoning: This was a large portion, but the Passover is the central unifying theme. Again, in big sections like this not every verse will be covered. But I chose the portions that best drove home the primary agenda, and I summarized other parts.

EXODUS 13:17–17:16

TS: Even though we persist in forgetting how good God is, He persists in his faithfulness to us.

Structure: *Inductive.* Moving through the episodes in these chapters, I allow our frustration with the Israelites to build by focusing on the verses that record their grumbling. Then I make the connection to us—we're the same. Eventually I reveal the complement that God persists in his faithfulness even when we don't. I do this by pointing out how in each episode God responds the same way—in grace. The complement does not take long to demonstrate from the passage, so I decided this structure would be most fitting.

OQ: How does God respond to persistent fear and grumbling?

Reasoning: I did not want to break this section into smaller chunks even though it is large. I saw a consistent theme of God providing miraculously over and over again through the Red Sea (chapter 14), which is the subject of Moses' song (chapter 15), the provision of sweet water from bitter water (end of 15), bread from heaven (16), water from a rock (first half of 17), and deliverance from the Amalekites (second half of 17). Again, rather than six sermons on essentially the same thesis, I chose to keep them together in one sermon. The tension in the text is the repeated griping and quarreling that the Lord responded to in grace. The grumbling is difficult to read until we realize we do the same thing. The resolution is that God is still that same God of grace. This theme unites this long preaching unit.

EXODUS 18

TS: God provides leaders in the church in order to guide us through the difficult Christian walk.

Structure: *Deductive*. I thought it wise to put the entire thesis statement out there as something for the listeners to contemplate, perhaps even feel uncomfortable with. Then as we move through the passage, we see the text making a case for the importance of leaders. Then I apply it carefully to our contemporary situation.

OQ: Are leaders really that crucial for me, for the church? What is the big deal? Isn't that an Old Testament thing?

Reasoning: Chapter demarcations do not always line up this nicely. Chapter 18 is an easy unit since it deals with Moses' judging of issues and Jethro's advice to recruit others so that Moses and the people are saved from being worn out.

EXODUS 19

TS: What we must realize about a mediated relationship with God is that it does not lower his standard of holiness.

Structure: *Deductive.* The passage starts out with the Lord affirming their relationship, but it hints at the contrast or distance between them early on (Moses has to go up and come down with the message, v. 3). Then the unapproachability of God ramps up from there, further driving home the complement.

OQ: But haven't we learned that he always responds in grace and persists in goodness even when we sin? Isn't God a loving Father who would hate to see us caught in legalism?

Reasoning: Another easy decision. Chapter 19 settles in nicely between chapters 18 and the beginning of the Decalogue in 20. The Israelites needed two provisions before they were ready to receive the law: a plurality of leadership in chapter 18 and a mountain experience in chapter 19. This chapter focuses on the unapproachable, fearsome God who is not to be treated lightly.

EXODUS 20:1–21

TS: We give God the honor he is due when we love him and love his children.

Structure: *Subject-Completed.* The Decalogue can be divided into two parts—a vertical table and a horizontal table. The first complement is borne out by verses 3–11 and the second by verses 12–17.

OQ: If God had a top ten list of ways to honor him, what would they be? What is it, at the most foundational level, that God expects from his worshippers?

Incremental Question (to set up complement #2): God himself wouldn't be loving if he did not teach us to love what he loves. We cannot love him if we do not love what he loves. What does God love that we must also love?

Reasoning: This section covers more than just the Ten Commandments proper. It is bracketed by verses 1–2 on the front end and verses 18–21 on the back end, which remind Israel that God is all-powerful and to be feared. Verses 22–26 begin a new section, which applies the Ten Commandments. The ten laws are prescriptive commands and what follows are lists of descriptive laws. Therefore, the cutoff point for this pericope is verse 21.

EXODUS 20:22–26

TS: Congregational worship must always be centered on the gospel to be appropriate before God.

Structure: *Inductive-Deductive.* I take the audience through the passage pointing out the curious demands that God makes—and they increase in their peculiarity. Then I reveal what God is getting at—he wants to protect the notion that he is the sole source of deliverance and not human hands. We desire to shape God into a manageable deity with whom we participate in deliverance. He will have none of it. That is the complement. Then I explain how the entire thesis pertains to our worship gatherings today.

OQ a: How do we know worship is appropriate? Is there such thing as inappropriate? How do we know when the line is crossed? **OQ b:** How do we protect God's sole boasting rights to deliverance and his unequaled status in our worship today?

Reasoning: The first table of the Decalogue is applied to altar construction here in verses 21:22–26. The second table is applied in the descriptive laws contained in verses 21:1–23:19. The first table is focused on our vertical relationship with the Lord while the second table is focused on our horizontal relationship with others. This distinction makes it easy to pick up on where to draw the line between each section.

EXODUS 21:1–23:9

TS: We need laws to teach us how to love our neighbor.

Structure: *Inductive-Deductive.* So many of these laws seem irrelevant to us today. I begin by agreeing that they seem foreign and outdated. I work my way to revealing the complement that they are about loving our neighbor. Then I proceed to explain, using examples from the text, how this is so.

OQ a: What are we supposed to do with all of these seemingly random and outdated laws? **OQ b:** How do these laws demonstrate how I can love my neighbor today?

Reasoning: The second table is applied via descriptive laws in verses 21:1–23:19. But I stopped it at verse 23:9 because I wanted to treat the Sabbath laws in their own sermon.

EXODUS 23:10–12

TS: We should honor the principle of the Sabbath in our Sunday worship because the principle behind the law is still good for us.

Structure: *Deductive.* For this one I come right out and say what I'm thinking: because we see the Sabbath commandment as an old covenant expectation, we tend to lose the value that it has pointed to all along. This is controversial and even serves as a correction to some who may be slack in their honoring of the Lord's Day, so there will be plenty of anticipation to see how I am going to make my case from the text.

OQ: Isn't the Sabbath done away with? Why honor it, but not other outmoded laws?

Reasoning: The Sabbath has come up several times now, and back in Exodus 20, I promised the congregation that we would unpack the fourth commandment more in an upcoming sermon.

In this message, I addressed the fourth commandment by surveying all the texts in Exodus on the Sabbath and then reminding them of the pattern of Creation in Genesis, as well as some verses in the New Testament that seem to speak to treating Sunday as a kind of Sabbath. This became a sort of textual-topical sermon where I begin with a passage, but the passage alone does not address all our concerns about the subject. So I put a case together from other passages as to how to understand it and apply it today.

EXODUS 23:20–33

TS: Our assurance of salvation is found in the fact that it is secured by Christ and marked by obedience.

Structure: *Subject-Completed.* I see two complements here, both emphasized roughly equally throughout the text. For this sermon I will cover one complement first, then move through the passage again emphasizing the other.

OQ: How can I know I am in a secure covenant relationship with God?

Incremental Question[111] (to set up Complement #2): But if it's all on Christ, doesn't that mean I can be lax in obedience?

---

111. For the subject-completed sermon, I use the term "incremental question," but in the two subject-completed examples included in this sermon series, you might wonder why they are not simply referred to as second overarching questions. The reason is that in an inductive-deductive sermon, there are two questions that overarch each structural half: one for the inductive portion and one for the deductive. Each portion answers a different question (thus, two OQs). In a subject-completed sermon, the OQ stays the same, but "incremental questions" bump us along from complement to complement. Each complement answers the same OQ, but there is more than one answer. In the two subject-completed sermons in this series, there are only two complements, but theoretically a subject-completed sermon can have any number of complements and therefore any number of incremental questions. But always one OQ.

Reasoning: This pericope bears two complements to the subject of the rescue of God's people. The first is that Christ secures it, and the second is that it is proven in obedience. The first complement is emphasized in the verses about how God is going to act through this angel who will lead them—he will get it done, not them (20, 23, 27–28, 31b). Yet the second complement is hard to miss. It is present in the verses that emphasize the required obedience that will not secure the covenant but rather must result from it (21–22, 23–24, 25, 32–33). I explain how the *if-then* language of the text does not undo this fact. During the explanation of the first complement, the case is made that, ultimately, the way God secures salvation for his people is in Christ. In the second complement, we see clearly from the text that faith produces works.

EXODUS 24:1–11

TS: To worship rightly, we must recognize that it cost Christ's life to make it possible.

Structure: *Inductive-Deductive.* I work my way from the first OQ to the complement after drawing the connection between the bloody rituals and Christ's spilled blood. Then from there I explain, from the rest of the verses, that the result of such a raw focus on sacrifice and blood does not lead to dour worship but to the contrary—it leads to a grand vision of God.

OQ a: What am I missing when I tend to worship flippantly or (conversely) with a guilt-stricken conscience? **OQ b:** Wouldn't it be too negative, gloomy, and depressing to always focus worship on sacrifice and death?

Reasoning: Since verse 24:12 begins a long chiasm all the way to verse 31:18 with the priesthood in the center, I decided that verses 24:1–11 function more as a prelude to that lengthy tabernacle section.

EXODUS 24:12–31:18

TS: We can be assured of our relationship with God because Jesus is our perfect priest.

Structure: *Inductive.* The full reveal that Jesus is the perfect fulfillment of the priesthood and the ministry of mediation will come after most of the exposition has been done, so this will work with an inductive approach.

OQ: How can I be assured I am in a relationship with God?

Reasoning: Alec Motyer provides a reasonably clear chiastic structure of this section where the function of the priesthood is in the middle.[112] While chiasms do not always necessarily work to emphasize the center portion as the central point, in this case it seems to work that way. Exodus greatly emphasizes God's distance, holiness, separation, and unapproachability. This section juxtaposes God's holiness with his initiative and desire for his people to commune with him. He accomplishes this via the priestly office.

EXODUS 32

TS: Sin is utterly destructive but God will not cast out the repentant.

Structure: *Inductive-Deductive*. This sermon massages the first OQ by seeing features in the text which demonstrate for us what sin is like. Then, once we recognize how devastating sin is and

---

112. J. A. Motyer, *The Message of Exodus: The Days of Our Pilgrimage* (Downers Grove, IL: InterVarsity Press, 2005), 253.

how easy it is to slip into rebellion, we see that there is hope because God rescues the repentant. The rest of the sermon proves that this hope is sure.

OQ a: Since sin is so pervasive and utterly destructive, what hope is there of our ever really coming out of it? **OQ b:** How do we know for sure that there is hope to come back from sin's devastation?

Reasoning: Following the chiastic structure of the previous unit and preceding the next unit, which is focused on Moses' making "atonement" for the rebellious people, this section focuses on the ugly nature of the rebellion in the golden calf incident.

EXODUS 33–40

TS: Our moral failures will not void God's presence with us because of Christ's intercession for the church.

Structure: *Inductive-Deductive*. In the introduction, I get them to the first OQ and then proceed to show how the Israelites were in this same predicament—a huge egregious failure that should have barred them from continuing on with God's presence. Then toward the middle of the sermon, I explain how it was Moses' intercession (and nothing else) that decisively turned God from rejection to continued presence. That reveals the complement that intercession is key. But whose? We don't have Moses today. Can a pastor do it? A parent? I draw the obvious connections to Jesus and explain that Christ's intercession for the Church secures God's presence, not our lack of failures.

OQ a: After a big moral failure, what guarantee is there that a walk with God can be continued? **OQ b:** I see that Moses' face-glowing intercession was effective for God's people then—what hope is there for me now?

Reasoning: This ends the series on a very large portion of Scripture, but it all coheres so well. The tabernacle construction in chapters 35–40 almost exactly repeats the tabernacle instructions given in chapters 25–30. The difference is that in chapters 25–30 the language was imperative—they had to build it. In chapters 35–40, the language is past—they *did* build it. In other words, all that was in danger, given Israel's sin, was rescued. The covenant remained intact. How? Intercession. Then this large section ends with 40:34–38, describing that indeed the Lord's glory remained with them wherever they went. While this proves to be a very similar thesis to the previous unit, the sermon feels different. The previous sermon spent the bulk of the time profiling what sin and rebellion looks like. This sermon lays heavy emphasis on how mediatory intercession secures God's presence even after rebellion.

APPENDIX C

Sample Sermon Outlines

The following sermons are intended to help you see what the principles in this book might look like when put into action. Each of the four sermon patterns discussed in this book are represented with explanatory comments where necessary. The thesis statement (TS) is provided for you in bold and I have italicized the various iterations of the overarching question (OQ). I have also put segues in angled brackets (<...>).

INDUCTIVE SERMON

This sermon is based on a short text, only two verses long. It was designed for the memorial service for a deceased believer. In this sermon, I eventually introduce the final two verses of the book in order to provide the author's clear answer to the OQ. The OQ is restated throughout, and then once the TS is revealed, it is repeated frequently so listeners leave without a doubt as to the answer. The last iteration of the TS contains the ultimate solution.

A GOOD NAME (ECCL 7:1–2)

Introduction

"A good name is better than precious ointment." This gem of a line comes to us from the middle of a sometimes neglected and often misunderstood book of the Bible. Ecclesiastes was written in raw fashion, designed to make you really think and take deep truths to heart. The author says, "A good name is better than precious ointment."

Nordstrom sells a cream by La Prairie called Cellular Cream Platinum Rare. They claim it's medicinal and can work wonders for your skin. It better! For a 1.7 oz. container, you're going to pay $1,200. How amazing can an ointment be?

"A good name is *better* than precious ointment." Better than money, good looks, massage therapy, age reversal ... better than any comfort in this life is *a good name*.

OQ (stated): *How do we get a good name? What makes a good name?* We gather today to remember ____________ of whom many of us would say, "Yes, _________ is a good name." But what makes that so? *What makes a good name?* The biblical author's answer may surprise you because he would probably differ from many of the reasons we might give.

<The author likes to leave things hanging out there for a while before providing his answer. So first we're going to see him deepen the question. His original readers, just like us, had to grapple with the weight of a name and *what makes it good*. But first he wants the question to really sink in further.>

I. What we need to understand first is that this question is more important than we realize.
   A. The full verse is found in Ecclesiastes 7:1 and goes like this: "A good name is better than precious ointment, and the day of death than the day of birth."

1. How in the world can the day of death be better than the day of birth?
2. When you witness birth, the name is just a name, a tag, what you're going to call them.
3. When you witness death, you know what their name means. Good or not.

B. When you choose a name for your baby, you instinctively go through this process.

1. If your spouse suggests a name and it reminds you of someone that really turns you off for whatever reason—you outright reject it, right?
2. Perhaps you choose a name that has the opposite effect—at the very least it doesn't remind you of someone who in your mind has made a bad name for themselves, but you might choose a name that has left a good impression on you through people that have made it a good name.

C. Choosing a name at the day of birth is important, but it is not until the day of death that you see what that person has done with that name.

D. The day of death is not more pleasant than the day of birth, but it brings out the importance of the question, *What makes a good name? What kind of name am I leaving?*

<Now it's as if the author is not satisfied yet. He's thinking, "No, you don't get it yet. You're not ready for the answer yet." We think, "What do you mean, c'mon, what's the answer—what makes a good name?" "No, you don't get it yet. You're not ready." This is his pattern throughout the whole book—pushing the question with stark sayings and observations about life that leave you desperate for relief. Look at how he ratchets up the question in the next verse.>

II. To understand how to answer this question, we need our perspective changed.
    A. Listen to the next verse: "It is better to go to the house of mourning than to go to the house of feasting" (paraphrase: It's better to go to a *funeral* than to a *feast*). Why? "For this is the end of all mankind, and the living will lay it to heart."
        1. Did you catch it? It's better to go to a funeral than a feast because we are all going to die someday. The funeral will make you discern that, whereas the feast will make you disregard it.
        2. At a feast we stuff ourselves with food and drink, we are focused on pleasure, good times, satiating our unmet desires with the delight of savory food, and medicating our pains with the suppression of drink. At such a feast, there is no meaning, there is no thought of what comes next or why anything is being done. There is only gratification and distraction.
        3. At a funeral, however, one is forced to confront the ultimate question: *What is the meaning of life?* One is forced to grapple with the idea that death "is the end of all mankind" and that "the living should take this to heart" (Eccl 7:2). The funeral serves as a splash of cold water for listless feast goers. It's a wake-up call for sleeping pleasure-seekers. Death arrests our attention and makes us ask, *What kind of name is* my *name? What does my name really mean—what is the meaning of the life I'm living? What is the "one thing" it's all really about?*

B. The point is well illustrated by this brief scene in the 1991 movie *City Slickers.*
   1. (Set up the plot and particular scene briefly.) Conversation between Mitch and Curly.

      Curly: D'ya know what the secret of life is?
      Mitch: (shrugs) No, what?
      Curly: This (holds up index finger.)
      Mitch: Your finger?
      Curly: One thing. Just one thing. You stick to that and everything else don't mean (squat).
      Mitch: That's great, but ... what's the one thing?
      Curly: That's what *you've* got to figure out.

   2. The movie takes Mitch through a series of events that brings him to find that his family is his "one thing."
   3. The writer of Ecclesiastes would have loved Curly's speech, but he would have given Mitch an F on his conclusion—it's the wrong answer.

C. The author tells us he's tried everything under the sun, and none of the things that we think could be life's one thing can ever possibly pass as suitable.
   1. He searched in vain for meaning in life. He looked for meaning in everything: money, friends, education, sex, children—you name it. He tried everything under the sun and found nothing that brings meaning to life.
   2. We tend to think that to make a good name you accomplish many things, you demonstrate generosity to those less fortunate than you, you

make a name for yourself by impressing people with what you've achieved or what you've accumulated. But it's all meaningless unless ...

<...unless you find the "one thing" that brings meaning. The one thing that makes a name any good at all. He gives us the answer. He mentions it in the middle of the book, but he drives it home clearly at the end.>

III. The author of Ecclesiastes answers the question with God.

- A. Ecclesiastes 12:13–14 reads: "The end of the matter; all has been heard. Fear God and keep his commandments, for this is the whole duty of man. For God will bring every deed into judgment, with every secret thing, whether good or evil."
    1. The whole duty of man is to fear God and obey him, to worship him and walk with him. THAT'S the one thing.
    2. He's saying, without God, death is meaningless because apart from God, *life* is meaningless.
    3. (Anticipated objection): "Lucas, I thought you said that witnessing a death is better than witnessing a birth because you are forced to evaluate your name. Now you're saying no matter what you do in life, it's all meaningless." No, it's all meaningless *without God*.
    4. **TS: The only way to leave behind a good name in this life is to live that life for God**. God takes everything we do, every action we take, whether public or private, and weighs it, judges it. Therefore, he is the one whose opinion counts. He is the judge of someone's name. **The only way to**

leave behind a good name in this life is to live that life for God. Fear him and obey him—this is your whole duty in life.

<Now if we leave here thinking we're going to go home and live better lives so that God will approve of our name, we are not on the right track yet. Good intention, but sadly it's not possible.>

IV. (Ultimate Solution) **We need Christ to make our name for us.**

A. None of us can truly make a good name for ourselves before God.

1. Our name only counts if we call upon one name—Jesus.
2. This is made plain in verses like Acts 4:12: "There is salvation in no one else, for there is no other name under heaven given among men by which we must be saved."
3. What we need to be saved from is not meaninglessness in general, but God's judgment specifically.
4. We all fall short of God's standard according to Romans 3:23. None of us can live lives that are ultimately meaningful because God will judge them as failed lives that fall short. And they do fall short.

B. But there is hope in Jesus Christ.

1. Jesus said, "I am the way, and the truth, and the life. No one comes to the Father except through me" (John 14:6).
2. Not *a* way, or *one* of many truths, or an *upgrade* to life. Rather, Jesus taught that he is the *only* way to come to the Father.

3. Though God is a judge, he is also a loving Father who has provided a way out of condemnation. Jesus took our judgement on the cross after living the good name none of us can live.
4. When we apply faith to Christ—we repent of our wayward living and we believe in the sufficiency of his substitution for us—then we are given his righteousness.
5. **A life lived in the righteousness of Jesus Christ himself—now that's a good name.**

CONCLUSION

The only way to leave behind a good name in this life is to live that life for God. We can be thankful to God that __________ has placed her faith in Christ and that whatever she did in this life will be judged by God not on her merits but on the merits of Jesus' own righteousness applied to her account. As we reflect on her life we reflect on ours. A time like this is a time to reckon with the big questions. To find the purpose of life, the center of meaning, the "one thing." A time like this is the opportune moment to make sure that Jesus secures the answer for you. By faith in Jesus Christ you can be ready for God's assessment of your life. Of your name. **Jesus is the only way to leave behind a good name in this life because only in Jesus can you live your life for God.**

DEDUCTIVE SERMON

This sermon serves as an introduction to an entire series through 1 Peter. The concept of suffering is not explicit in the first two verses, but it is a primary theme in the epistle and the concept of "exiles" introduces it.

LIVING AS EXILES (1 PET 1:1–2)

Introduction

One reality that Jesus made plain to his disciples is that following Christ guarantees you will be an outsider in this world and you will not be liked for it. "In this world you will have tribulation" (John 16:33). "If you were of the world, the world would love you as its own; but because you are not of the world, but I chose you out of the world, therefore the world hates you" (15:19).

We may not feel like this is exactly our experience today where we live, but that's not because Jesus was wrong. We need to evaluate whether we're really following Christ if we're not feeling any pressure because of it. We live, here and now, in an increasingly hostile environment. If you are loud about Jesus, you're going to feel like you don't belong. How will you bear up when pressure gets intense?

You might work in an environment where being Christlike puts you at a disadvantage; you're expected to conform to unbiblical standards. You might receive pressure from an unbelieving spouse, an unbelieving professor, an unbelieving friend. After a while it gets tiresome. We look to Jesus and he tells us to expect worse. How do we endure it? Some of us may feel like the pressure is already too much. Others of us look to our brothers and sisters in other parts of the world whose lives are in danger because of their faith in Christ and we doubt we would ever be able to withstand that kind of persecution. Would we?

<First Peter was written to address exactly this reality for Christians. Peter writes to address suffering due to being a Christian. Now, since this is Peter writing, this letter is dated *before* persecution of Christianity was made official by Rome. They were not necessarily dealing with beatings or jail time—but

they were dealing with at least the kinds of things we deal with: maligning, slander, unfair treatment, ostracism. Being a kind of social outcast threatened their livelihood, their standing in the community, not to mention heat from their own families. Peter writes to address this, and he reveals his main point right off the bat in his opening lines. **TS: We can endure suffering for being a Christian by understanding that we are chosen by God.** (Restate): **We can live as foreigners in this world by recognizing that we enjoy a sovereign election by God.** Let's look at the first two verses together.>

OQ: (implied) *What does my election have to do with enduring suffering?* Or *I'm not sure I believe in election; I'm not sure that's a biblical concept.*

(Read verses 1–2.)

I. Peter wants us to start with our identity.
   A. Before getting into how Christians are to respond to and live under the world's oppression, he begins with their identity.
   B. He's saying: "It's who you are that will define how you live and respond."
   C. More than just a cursory greeting, these first two verses define the Christian's identity, couched completely in the work of the Triune God.
   D. The important truth about Christianity that we must not overlook or underestimate is we are saved completely by God—chosen by him, set apart by him, brought into a covenant relationship with him and by him.
   E. This is the truth that must be understood in order for the epistle to make sense: **We are chosen by God for a complete salvation.**

<Let's look at some of the details of the text so we can get a grasp on why this truth should be a source of encouragement and endurance for us.>

II. We are exiles in this world.

- A. Exiles can be translated "foreigners" or "strangers" (v. 1).
- B. The idea is that we do not belong to this world, we have no citizenship here, no rights or privileges.
- C. "Dispersion" sets up the analogy with the Jewish Diaspora after the Babylonian captivity—Babylon took over and as a result Israelites were scattered all over, pushed out of their land, now living in places where they are foreigners who don't belong.
- D. Peter is setting them up for the idea that "of course you'll have suffering—you don't belong here, you are foreign to this place."

<But it is not simply the concept of exile that is encouraging. In fact, you may find that quite *dis*couraging. It is. But it is the *kind* of exiles we are that is of great encouragement.>

III. We are *elect* exiles (v. 1).

- A. "Elect" is not a word that belongs exclusively to one theological camp. It's a biblical word.
- B. "Elect" or "chosen" contrasts with the concept of exiles because with respect to God we are anything but foreign.
- C. That is, you have a vertical situation that contrasts greatly with your horizontal situation.
- D. What this letter will make clear is that your vertical situation defines how you handle your horizontal situation.

E. Notice that the letter opens and closes with the "chosen" concept (5:13)—it is meant to be your primary source of hope.

<Election is a concept that we tend to underappreciate regardless of how comfortable we are with the term. But Peter wants to boost your appreciation of this doctrine because without it, you will struggle in your exile. So he uses three phrases to describe this election with each enacted by a person of the Trinity. With each, you will grow in your appreciation of election and what it means for your exile.>[113]

IV. We are chosen according to the foreknowledge of God (v. 2).

A. The word "chosen" here can mean simply knowledge of the future, but that is not likely the meaning here.

1. Twice in the New Testament the word clearly means an intellectual knowledge of something, and both times it refers to humans. The other times refer to God, in which case I believe it means more than just prior knowledge of what is going to happen.

<Give me a few minutes to make this case because I think it's important.>[114]

---

113. These three phrases could possibly be set up as three complements if the subject is election. But I chose to go with a straight deductive pattern with encouragement in suffering as the subject and election as the complement. Thus I see these three phrases are explanations or proofs of the complement and not separate complements on their own.

114. This portion takes the form of a doctrinal sermon where other passages are introduced to clarify a point of truth that is not fully borne out in the immediate text. With a sticky doctrine like election, this can be necessary especially for my audience, and with a short two-verse text, there is room to do it.

2. "Know" in the Bible often means relational knowing, not intellectual knowing.
    a. In Amos 3:2, the Lord says to Israel, "You only have I known among all the families of the earth." Does God not know the other nations? Of course he knows them, but he doesn't have a *relationship* with them.
    b. In Matthew 7, Jesus tells the unrepentant, "I never knew you." Same concept.
    c. Galatians 4:9 says, "Now that you have come ... to be known by God." They were known before; it's the relationship that is new.
    d. 1 Corinthians 8:3 says, "If anyone loves God, he is known by God." He knows those who love him in a way that he doesn't know everyone else—he is in a covenant relationship with them.

B. God's foreknowledge doesn't refer to prediction but providence.
1. 1 Peter 1:20 (display on screen)—it doesn't make sense to think that God first consults what he sees himself doing before he ordains himself to do it. Instead, it means that before the foundation of the world, he chose to make Christ Redeemer.
2. Romans 11:2 (display on screen)—it's not a very powerful point to say, "Of course God won't reject Israel, because he already *sees* (predicts) that they won't be rejectable!" Rather, the point is quite the opposite. As much as Israel rejects God, God will not reject Israel, *providentially* keeping for himself a remnant of believers by his grace only.

3. Acts 2:23 (display on screen)
    a. Who delivered Christ up? God did.
    b. How would it help Peter's case to say God *saw* it and planned accordingly? If it's already going to happen, why plan? It means the reverse: God planned it, so it happened accordingly.
4. God is not just rubber-stamping what he sees happening already; he makes things happen.
5. Foreknowledge in 1 Peter 1:2 means that **God chose beforehand to make a relationship with his people.**

<When we undervalue this doctrine, we overvalue our own ability to withstand the pressures of living as unwelcome exiles. But God's election is not just about a final destination; it's about our holiness. The character that we need to endure our exile is given to us.>

V. We are made holy by the Holy Spirit (v. 2).
    A. To sanctify means to be made holy.
    B. This isn't referring to the process of sanctification so much as the fact that we have been transformed.
    C. We were unholy and God has made us holy—HE has done it.
    D. **What we need to endure suffering for being a Christian is given to us by the Holy Spirit in election.**

<So Peter is moving our confidence from ourselves, or from wherever else we may misplace our confidence, and centering it on the accomplished work secured for us in election. He doesn't want you to doubt your endurance under pressure. And if you know Christ—if you are *known by* Christ—you shouldn't doubt

the strength that he has granted you in your exile. Frankly, when we doubt it, it's because we don't appreciate the gospel—Christ's work on our behalf.>

VI. (Ultimate Solution) **You can endure exile because you are brought into a covenant relationship by Christ's sacrifice.**

A. Exodus 24 provides the background to this phrase: Moses read the book of the covenant to the Israelites, and they vowed obedience, then he sprinkled them with the sacrificed blood.

B. In other words, obedience is a part of the covenantal relationship, but it would not be possible if Christ did not provide it with his blood.

C. God doesn't call you to endure the wilderness of this world without supplying you with what you need for it—a secure and transformative relationship with him.

<Peter writes this knowing the pressure you face or that you will face. He failed when he didn't think he would fail, denying Jesus just after claiming he would follow him to the death. He knows how frail we can feel in our exile, standing up for Jesus when Jesus is not around. But this letter is meant to encourage you, not by softening the hard realities that exile can bring, but by building up your understanding of election.>

VII. **We can endure suffering for being a Christian by understanding that we are chosen by God.**

A. Peter introduces the letter like this because the way to not feel overwhelmed by our exile is to understand that our election is accomplished by God.

B. It is ultimately a work of the Father, the Son, and the Holy Spirit—not us.

C. That means that it is effective, and, therefore, it is comforting.
D. You are an exile in this place, yes, but it is temporary and you have been chosen to endure it.

CONCLUSION

We can rest in the fact that the Father has chosen us, the Spirit has sanctified us, and through the work of Jesus, we are brought into a relationship of obedience. Family, it's going to be tough out there. Understand that **God has chosen you, completely saved you. While you don't belong to this world, you belong to him, and that should encourage you in difficult times.**

INDUCTIVE-DEDUCTIVE SERMON

THE UNSEEN CHRIST (MARK 8:1–30)

Introduction

Most of you can name at least one person in your life that has been exposed to clear, repeated presentations of the gospel and have yet to confess Christ. Lots of people around you have heard about the gospel, but this particular category of person has high exposure. Clear and repeated exposure to the gospel. Maybe you've been the one repeating it to them over and over. They understand it, they could probably explain it, but they just don't believe it. Your heart aches for them. Their resolute unbelief is frustrating.

OQ: *How can people see that Jesus is the answer to their deepest need? How can these impossible people ever really see the gospel?*

We want them to come to Christ so desperately because we love them. But they just don't get it. What do we pin our hopes to? Explain the gospel a little more clearly? Invite them to church when an especially gifted preacher is in town? Give them a book that might persuade them? What can we do to get them to see the gospel, to really understand it, to truly see it?

All those evangelistic endeavors are great and needed. But we can't pin our hopes to any of them. There's one factor that really matters.

<In the Gospel of Mark, the eighth chapter, we're going to see the same dilemma: people who receive especially clear and repeated exposure to the gospel and miss it. Before we see the one factor that can change it, Mark is going to present the problem in stark relief: the sad reality that people can hear the gospel but be deaf to it, see the gospel clearly presented but be blind to it. Please turn with me to Mark chapter 8 and we'll begin at verse 1.>

I. Jesus demonstrates that he is the answer to our deepest need, but this truth is shockingly easy to miss. (Read verses 1–9.)[115]
   A. If this were a TV show you were watching, you'd pause it right here and ask, "Wait a minute—didn't we see this episode already?" This text seems so familiar because we just covered a very similar event in chapter 6 a few weeks ago.

---

115. Often, especially when I am reading longer portions of text in one shot, I will insert clarifying comments here and there to help listeners stay with the reading. I might mention the fact that the people were starved for food and ask them if they've ever felt three-day hunger before. I might make a point about Jesus' deep compassion for the crowd where he sees the need and it unsettles him. I'll emphasize words like "seven baskets full" and "satisfied" and describe what that would look like today. These are quick comments to help clarify the reading, but their brevity and their pithiness helps keep them with me throughout the reading of a chunk of verses. Later, when I connect hunger to our eternal hunger, and Jesus' compassion toward us in his satisfying our need, it will have been helpful to the listeners that I underscored those portions of the reading.

    1. There are many similarities between this feeding miracle and the previous one, but also several differences (list a few examples).
    2. This is important to note because while the differences confirm that it is not the same event, the similarities emphasize a lesson that is yet to be learned for the disciples and for the reader.

B. Jesus is the answer to our deepest need, our most basic hunger.

C. But it doesn't look like the disciples are quite grasping who they're dealing with in Jesus.
    1. They either don't seem to recall the previous miracle feeding.
    2. Or, perhaps they assume that Jesus can't or won't do it again.
    3. But they actually say, "How can one feed these people with bread here in this desolate place?" Seriously? We've been here before.
    4. With the seven baskets left over, Jesus demonstrates once again that he can more than satisfy the hunger of the people.
    5. But the disciples, as much as they like Jesus and desire to follow him, simply *miss* what Jesus is getting at—they are missing the gospel.

<Maybe the person you're thinking of that just cannot see the truth no matter how exposed they are to it are like the disciples. They miss the obvious no matter how obvious. You might be tempted to think, "If only God would do a *really* obvious work in their lives, they might come awake and follow Jesus. If Jesus would show himself to them in a can't-ignore-it, supernatural

way, they would have no choice but to believe. Right?" No, my friend, this thinking is misguided. No matter what is done to demonstrate the gospel, if they won't see it, they won't see it. Some people *demand* a sign from God to prove Jesus' gospel claim to them. But it won't work.

Look at how the next three verses describe this kind of group.>

II. Not even a clear sign from heaven will convince the unbeliever of the gospel. (Read verses 10–13.)
   A. Consider what Jesus has already done that Mark has recorded up to this point.
      1. He's cast out unclean spirits. "What if there's an entire legion of them?" Doesn't matter.
      2. He's lifted fevers and all manner of diseases including leprosy with a touch.
      3. He's reversed paralysis and un-crippled the crippled.
      4. He's calmed the sea; he's walked on the sea.
      5. He raised a dead girl back to life.
      6. Many of these things the Pharisees have witnessed firsthand.
      7. Now, for the second time, he has fed multiple thousands with food that was only enough for one or two people.
   B. But the miracles they've either heard of or witnessed are not enough. They want something that requires no interpretation, something clear, something incontrovertible.
   C. Jesus denies them.
      1. He's exasperated with their stubbornness (v. 12a).
      2. He says, "No you're not going to get a sign from heaven" (v. 12b).

3. They probably wanted something akin to the signs of confirmation we see in the OT, such as fire from heaven or some apocalyptic demonstration.
4. A sign would be worthless because they won't see it.
5. If Jesus provides one sign, they'll want another. If Jesus fixes one problem, they'll want the next problem fixed before they commit. Or they won't attribute it to Jesus and they'll explain it away. It never ends.
6. You cannot gain by evidence what can only be received by faith.

D. As much as we are desperate to see our loved ones saved, praying for God to show up in a big way in their lives to "prove" himself to them is probably not the focus we need to have. It doesn't work that way.

<If repeated exposure to the gospel won't do it, and a clear sign from heaven won't do it, what should we look to for hope? We don't understand what they need because we often forget what their real problem is. It's a universal problem we all share. Watch Mark bring this to light:>

III. Jesus exposes the problem that we all share. (Read verses 14–21.)

A. Bread becomes the focus again, showing that verses 10–13 was not Mark moving on from the second bread miracle—it's all tied together. He's still getting to the bottom of the problem: *Why do people miss Jesus even when he's right in front of them?*

B. The plight is universal, and this is seen in the fact that the disciples are in danger of the same problem that has infected the Pharisees.

1. By leaven/yeast, Jesus was referring to the *teaching* of the Pharisees (Matt 16:12). He was referring to their *hypocrisy* (Luke 12:2). But what does their teaching and hypocrisy have in common with Herod?
2. Simply put, both were too hardened to believe. They suffered from unbelief, and Jesus is warning the disciples that this disease is a danger for them too.
3. The inability to really grasp what Jesus was getting at with the bread is due to hardness of the heart. Mark makes that clear in verse 6:52.

C. The reason repeated gospel presentations just keep bouncing off our lost loved ones, the reason even a sign from heaven would not work to change them, the reason they persist in their unbelief is because they are hardened.

   1. Another word for hardened is "blind"—this is why Jesus calls them both hardened (v. 17) and unable to see (v. 18).
   2. They can't understand the gospel because they can't really see it.
   3. The gospel can be communicated logically and compellingly, but it doesn't compute because *they can't see*.

D. **TS**: *How can people see that Jesus is the answer to their deepest need?* Friends, listen: **The only way anyone can come to truly know that Jesus is the satisfying answer to their deepest hunger is for Jesus to grant them the ability to see it.**

<When Jesus ends his speech with, "Do you not yet understand?," the conversation for Mark isn't over. He wants you to see that

Jesus is now going to do something that demonstrates the truth he's after this entire time: **The gospel can only be seen when Jesus grants the ability to see it.** For Mark, Jesus is saying, "Do you not understand? Of course you don't. But let me show you what I am going to do about that." And he heals a blind man to show it.>

IV. Jesus can reverse our blindness. (Read verses 22–26.)

   A. This episode is an illustration of the previous paragraphs: The Pharisees and Herod are unable to see Jesus for who he really is. The disciples are in danger of staying stuck in the same unbelief. The blind man cannot see ... until he is *made to see* by God.

   B. It's a curious thing that in this one miracle, Jesus heals in two stages.

      1. Did he not get it right the first time?
      2. Is Jesus losing his touch a bit? Running out of power?
      3. No, I think the sequential nature of this healing matches what it is meant to illustrate: the sequential removal of blindness from the disciples' eyes.
      4. They are starting to get it now, but they won't fully get it until Christ is resurrected.
      5. That doesn't mean we get saved gradually, no. But it does mean that often times the unbeliever goes through phases of disbelief morphing into questioning disbelief and then plausible belief and then, "Wait a minute, I've really got to think about this."

   C. But don't miss the obvious point: **Jesus must grant sight to the blind in order for the blind**

to see the gospel. No one is going through any phases toward sight unless Jesus does it.

D. You might say, "Now wait a minute—you mean to tell me that if I don't believe the gospel that it's simply a matter of God not giving me the sight of faith? That it's not my fault?" No, we are guilty for our blindness—it is a self-willing blindness.

1. This is why Jesus pleads with them with a string of eight questions:
   - Why are you discussing the fact that you have no bread?
   - Do you not yet perceive or understand?
   - Are your hearts hardened?
   - Having eyes do you not see, and having ears do you not hear?
   - And do you not remember?
   - When I broke the five loaves for the five thousand, how many baskets full of broken pieces did you take up?
   - And the seven for the four thousand, how many baskets full of broken pieces did you take up?
   - Do you not yet understand?
2. You can hear that Jesus *expects* them to see and understand, to believe. Yet at the same time, he is teaching that they do not have the ability to do it. They love their blindness; it's a welcome yeast.

E. (Ultimate Solution) **What hope do any of us have to believe? We need the work of God.**

1. A work we cannot merit, a work we cannot even co-produce. God must cause us to see. God must reveal to us the reality of the gospel of Jesus.

2. We are all lost, starved, dying people with no satisfaction and no hope of resolving this ourselves.
3. Jesus, through his life, death, resurrection, and ascension to the Father secures for us the eternal bread we need for infinite satisfaction—Jesus himself.
4. If we repent of our willing blindness and our love of sin, and we place faith in Christ for salvation, then we will be saved.
5. This is what happens when we see.

<Many of us spend time trying to convince our loved ones of the gospel—this is good and responsible—but they cannot be convinced by reasoning or evidences. Not ultimately. Mark drives home a final nail to make sure we don't miss this.>

V. Peter's confession is a result of God's work on his heart and nothing else. (Read verses 27–30.)
   A. In Matthew 16:17, Jesus tells Peter he is able to make this confession because the Father has revealed it to him.
      1. He didn't "figure it out."
      2. He didn't simply become convinced by compelling outward evidence.
      3. It was revealed to him.
      4. At first when I read this in my preparation time I thought, "Well, this isn't Matthew, this is Mark—if Mark wanted us to see that Peter was only able to see because the Father granted it to him, then he would've said so."
      5. But he did—in the account of Jesus giving the blind man sight. Peter is the blind man beginning to see things, though not completely.

6. We all, like Peter, like the blind man, need the veil lifted in order to see.

B. All these verses work together to drive this point home.
   1. In the miracle of the bread and fish, Jesus is telling the disciples, "I am the bread that starving people need and I can satisfy them, don't you see it?"
   2. In the miracle of healing the blind man, Jesus is telling his disciples, "The reason you don't see it is because you're blind. But I can fix that for you."
   3. **Unbelievers will only see Jesus as their answer when God in Christ Jesus through the ministry of the Holy Spirit removes their blindness to the gospel.**

C. It is not that we are uninvolved in the process.
   1. God *uses* evangelism, apologetics, conversations, sermons, and the like.
   2. We must be intentional witnesses, and like Paul, we try to persuade.
   3. But, also like Paul, we recognize that in the end, it's not about words of eloquent wisdom. It's about the demonstration of the Spirit's power.
   4. This power is the unique ability God has to lift blindness.
   5. We need to remain involved in the process but with a different focus.
   6. Rather than trying harder to convince our loved ones, we should intercede for them more fervently, more frequently, more confidently.
   7. We need to place our confidence in what only God can do rather than leaning on what our efforts cannot do.

CONCLUSION

Jesus shows that he is the answer to our deepest need, and he also shows that he provides the way to *see it*. **Your cousin, your roommate, your spouse, your child, will never see Jesus through arm-twisting, logical argumentation, or pleading.** They will only see Jesus if Jesus touches their blind eyes to give them sight. **Then they will see he is what they are so desperately craving.**

The answer isn't to quit witnessing or to stop sharing our faith. On the contrary, we persist, but with a well-placed confidence. Our hope is in God's work of giving sight to the blind. So we spread the gospel out like the bread and fish to the crowds. We tell the crowds that there is hope for their lost-ness, their separation from God, their deepest hunger. We tell them they need Jesus. **We share the gospel of Jesus, but only Jesus can make them see it.**

SUBJECT-COMPLETED SERMON

All throughout this series in Exodus, I had been emphasizing the parallel between Israel's bondage/wilderness/promised land experience with our salvation experience. I made this case in the introductory sermon, as you can see in Appendix B. Thus the connection is not proven in this sermon but largely assumed.

HE WILL LEAD YOU (EXOD 23:20–33)

Introduction

If something, God forbid, were to happen to you tonight that claimed your life, where would you go? Jesus talks about dividing the sheep and the goats, those who follow him and those who don't—there are two camps, two destinations. Which one are you in? Are you sure?

Too many churchgoers today still answer with performance—they go to church, they read the Bible, they help others less fortunate than themselves, they live good moral lives. But that's not an answer. Lots of goats live like that. What makes me a sheep, shepherded by Christ? It's not doing good works because we could never be sure that way, could we? How many good works does it take to make me a legitimate Christian? How many good deeds does it take to compensate for all of my bad deeds? How many bad deeds am I even really aware of? Even if I knew the ratio, how could I ever be sure I'm aware of my complete list of sins? What if some of my good deeds I only did out of a selfish motive to compensate for bad deeds so that I can be in the clear? Do those count as "good"?

It's only confusing if we've got Christianity all wrong. It saddens me when I hear Christians asked if they know they are going to heaven and they say something like, "Well, I sure hope so!" I understand the sentiment of wanting to appear humble. But it's the wrong answer.

So here's the question, put another way:

> **OQ:** *How can I know I am in a secure covenant relationship with God?*

<Exodus may seem like an unlikely place to turn to answer that question, but this is a passage where we'll see that God's answer to this has always been the same. We're in chapter 23, and what we see here is God has rescued his people from bondage. They have this conquest of the promised land ahead of them, and he is giving them what they need to make it. The question is surely ringing in their minds and hearts, "Are we going to make it?" And God wants to assure them. He wants to assure *us*. Let's take a look beginning in verse 20.>

TEXT: Exodus 23:20–33 (Read all.)[116]

I. **TS (first complement):** Immediately we see that **their covenant life is <u>secured</u> by the *Lord's leadership*.**
   A. As a part of their covenant relationship with the Lord, they are to take the promised land.
      1. It is the same as our march toward the promised land in that it is not secured by our work ethic.
      2. Consider that they are *already in* the covenant before God even gave them the law—the covenant relationship from the beginning is based on grace not merit.
      3. The rest of the Bible bears this out—OT and NT.
   B. I do not want you to go home today paranoid that there's no way to be sure you're going to make it.
   C. Look at how this passage emphasizes the Lord's role in the success of his people:
      1. (v. 20) "When my angel goes before you ... and *I* blot them out"—the Lord is sending them on the conquest, but he is the one making it succeed.
      2. (vv. 27–28) "I will send my terror before you ... and I will make ..."—they won't be afraid of you because of you, but they'll be afraid of you because of *me*.
      3. (v. 31) "I will give the inhabitants of the land into your hand"—how do they get the land? Simply put: because God gives it to them.

---

116. Because I won't be moving through the verses in a linear fashion for this sermon, it benefits the listeners to read it through together with me, uninterrupted except for very brief explanatory comments. They are with me because they are looking for the relevance to the OQ and they are seeing glimmers of it in the reading, but are anxious to hear me unpack it to get the answer they are looking for.

What secures our relationship in this covenant with God is God's leadership.

D. (Ultimate Solution) More specifically, **we make it to the end because God provides Christ to lead us.**
   1. He sends an angel before them to lead them (vv. 20–23).
   2. Briefly, many Christians believe when this angel of the Lord appears, it is the Son of God.
      a. "The angel of the LORD" in the OT would speak on behalf of God and is identified with God.
      b. This is why, for example, we see the angel of the Lord appear in the burning bush and tell Moses, "I am the God of your father" (3:6).
      c. Here in Exodus 23 we see God say that this angel of the Lord has the power to forgive or withhold forgiveness, "for my name is in him" (v. 21).
      d. And, of course, we know that this is true of our faith. Jesus is the one who goes out in front and leads us—he authors and perfects our faith so we look to him (Heb 12:2).
   3. We don't have to simply shrug and say, "I hope so" when we're asked about the ultimate success of our covenant relationship with God—our entrance into the far greater land of promise—not because we're sure of ourselves but because we're sure of Christ's leadership.

<Now, the temptation here is to think, "If my eternity with the Lord is secured for me by Christ, then doesn't that mean I can be lax in my obedience?" Many Christians deny the

sovereign role Christ plays in our final deliverance because of that precise objection. Yet, while the covenant is secured by the Lord's leadership, it is marked by radical obedience. You don't secure your destination with God by obedience; the security is provided by Christ's leading us. But that security is shown, demonstrated, marked by a life of zealous obedience to Christ.>

II. **TS (second complement): The covenant life is marked by *radical obedience*** (vv. 21–22, 23–24, 25, 32–33).

- A. Your relationship with the Lord is not secured by a spiritual work ethic, but it is *proven* by it—thus obedience is demanded:
    1. (v. 21) "Pay careful attention to him and obey his voice."
    2. (v. 22) "But if you carefully obey his voice and do all that I say."
    3. (v. 24) "You shall not ... but you shall ... "
    4. (v. 25) "You shall serve the LORD your God."
    5. (vv. 32–33) "You shall make no covenant with them and their gods."
- B. Don't get stuck on the "if-then" language (v. 23).
    1. Jesus uses it too:
        - a. Matthew 6:14–15, "If you forgive others their trespasses, your heavenly Father will also forgive you, but if you do not forgive others their trespasses, neither will your Father forgive your trespasses."
        - b. Humanly speaking it plays out this way, but that's not how it works in the literal sense.
        - c. Same here in Exodus—if someone does not obey the covenant, then they don't have the

faith that makes them a real covenant member, and this is shown in their disobedience.

C. (Ultimate Solution) **If someone is not sure if they are in a relationship with God or if they are going to persevere to the end, the answer is not to obey more. The answer is to place your faith and trust in Jesus Christ as your only Mediator.**

D. But the *sign* that someone has not done that would be a life marked by disobedience.

E. This is what James was writing about:
   1. A faith without works isn't a saving faith (2:14).
   2. Faith is proven by works (2:18).
   3. The Bible is consistent on this matter.

F. **We make it because the Lord leads us and this is shown in radical obedience.**

<Why do I say *radical* obedience?>

III. What God demands is careful obedience (1–2).

A. (v. 21) "Pay *careful* attention to him and obey his voice"—could be translated "*guard* your attention to him."

B. Notice the contrast: outright rebellion ("do not rebel against him," v. 21), or careful, idol-smashing obedience (v. 24).

C. We introduce this category of lazy, casual obedience, but the Bible has no place for it.

D. **If we are in a secured relationship with God, then it will show itself in a radical, zealous, guarded obedience to him.**

<Think about how this should look in our lives. What are we to take the most care about? What are we to carefully guard against?>

IV. Radical obedience means we guard against sneaky idolatry.
   A. We may think, "I don't have idols," but look at why they would serve idols:
      1. The idols would represent deities in charge of agriculture/crops.
      2. The idols would represent deities in charge of fertility/children.
      3. The idols would represent deities in charge of health/long life.
      4. The temptation has always been to serve alternative sources of security rather than the Lord who promises he is the Source (vv. 25–26).
   C. We disobey by serving other sources of security besides the Lord.
      1. Our job—we sideline spiritual disciplines, like time in the word, time in fellowship for the sake of work, work, work.
      2. Our family—we're afraid to restrict our kids' freedom because we don't want them to rebel, but in our lack of parenting, we disobey the Lord. We put their sports before church. When we move, we look at school districts, but we don't look at what congregation we would be plugging them in to.
      3. Our health—we go to doctors, therapists, or personal trainers before we go to the Lord with things. We spend more time with consultants than we do in prayer. What do our priorities say of what we think about the Lord's role in providing what we need?

D. It is alluring to prioritize other sources of security before the Lord, but it's a trap!
   1. "If you serve their gods, it will surely be a snare to you" (v. 33).
   2. It is so easy to serve the benefits instead of the Benefactor.
   3. Disobedience never pays—a life of disobedience only serves to display your lack of faith in Christ.

E. But if you have repented and placed your faith in Jesus Christ, then your relationship with the Lord is *secured by his leadership* and *marked by your obedience*.

CONCLUSION

Christ is our guide and he will lead us home. There is security in that. But if we look for security in other sources, that is a sign that we might not be in a relationship with God because he doesn't share that spot. **Place your hope of the "promised land" in Christ's secure leadership, and let it result in a life marked by radical obedience**.

Author/Subject Index

Scripture Index